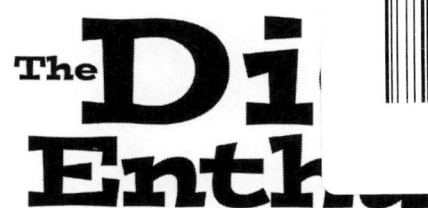

Book Three   January 2016

Cover		Joe Wehrle, Jr.
	2	Editor's Notes
Interview	4	Heather Jacobs: *Big Fiction*
Review	12	Ron Fortier's Pulp Fiction Reviews
Art	17	Brad Foster's Guest of Honor artwork for Worldcon 2015
Article	18	Beyond the Borderline by Tom Brinkmann
Article	31	*Dope Fiends* Trading Cards
Fiction	34	Planetstorm story and art by Joe Wehrle, Jr.
Review	39	*A Blonde for Murder* by Walter B. Gibson
Article	42	The Horror of the Creeping Monsters by Peter Enfantino
Synopses	48	*Super-Science Fiction* by Peter Enfantino
Review	66	*Popular Fiction Periodicals* by Jeff Canja
Article	70	Diabolik-al Digests by Joe Wehrle, Jr
Fiction	75	The Rail City Rolls by Ron Fortier
Review	81	*Betty Fedora* #2
Article	84	The Dashiell Hammett Digests by Steve Carper
Biblio	101	Dashiell Hammett Digest Bibliography by Steve Carper
Review	103	*Paperback Parade* #89
Profile	106	"Mr. UFO" Timothy Green Beckley's Paranormal Odyssey by Tom Brinkmann
Review	119	*Manhunt* December 1953
Fiction	122	Old Aunt Sin by Gary Lovisi, Art: Michael Neno
Review	131	*Children's Digest* Spring 1972
Review	132	*Fate* #727
Article	136	*Gunsmoke* by Peter Enfantino
	148	Social Intercourse: Letters and social media roundup
	151	Opening Lines

Editor/Publisher/Designer Richard Krauss   Contributing Editor D. Blake Werts
Cartoons by Brad Foster and Bob Vojtko

Visit us online at larquepress.com/blog for current and vintage digest covers and news. Join our privacy-secure mailing list, used exclusively for updates on *The Digest Enthusiast* and Larque Press at larquepress.com

The Digest Enthusiast (TDE) Book Three, Jan 2016. © 2016. Contributors retain copyright for content contributed. TDE aspires to quarterly publication by Larque Press LLC, 6327 SW Capitol Highway, Suite C #293, Portland, Oregon 97239. All rights reserved. Unauthorized reproduction in any manner, other than excerpts in fair use, is prohibited.

Note: Scanned covers that appear in TDE are retouched to remove tears or other defects from the original source. When reference material is not available, retouched areas are "best guess."

Editor's Notes

I prefer to buy my favorite digest magazines at the newsstand. These days, that requires a special trip and in some cases special effort. Digests, along with the whole magazine industry, face sales and distribution challenges. But there is a bright spot on the virtual magazine rack. Short run and print-on-demand digests seem to be appearing in greater number and offer readers a chance to discover new favorites, available direct or online.

Contributing editor D. Blake Werts starts off *TDE3* with an interview with Heather Jacobs, editor of *Big Fiction*, a recently minted digest, dedicated to long form stories. You'll also find reviews of an old favorite, *Paperback Parade*, and a new one, *Betty Fedora*, in this edition. When you hear about a new digest magazine, or have one you'd like to see us highlight, drop me a line (arkay@larquepress.com). Part of our mission is to unite the community of readers and collectors and build awareness for new digest magazines.

I'm thrilled to welcome several new contributors to this issue. Steve Carper brings us the history and bibliography of Dashiell Hammett's work in digests, and insight into his publishing relationship with Frederick Dannay (half of the Ellery Queen duo).

Peter Enfantino provides two comprehensive retrospectives. The first covers the complete eighteen-issue run of the giant monster favorite, *Super-Science Fiction*. His second examines the short-lived western companion to Flying Eagle's *Manhunt*, called *Gunsmoke*.

I first became aware of New Pulp champion Ron Fortier in the 1970s. We both were contributors to Gordon Linzner's SF Zine *Space and Time* in that era. Years later I rediscovered Ron's writing and publishing work through his online presence. When the opportunity to include his work here came up, it was an occasion too good to pass up.

Brad Foster was one of the Guests of Honor at "Sasquan," the Worldcon 2015 held in Spokane, Washington last August. He created a special illustration used for the event and graciously allows us to run it here, along with several cartoons you'll find throughout the

Editor's Notes

issue. Cartoonist Bob Vojtko also contributes a set of brand new 'toons for the issue.

Joe Wehrle, Jr. returns with a stellar new cover for this edition. His article on the Italian comics digest *Diabolik* includes portraits of the lead characters and the two women who created Diabolik along with many of his early adventures. Joe also brings us his latest science fiction yarn: "Planetstorm."

Tom Brinkmann follows up his article last time on *Borderline*, with a "companion piece" about *Beyond: Documented Truth About the Strange Phenomena of Our Times*. He also provides a profile on one of *Beyond*'s contributors, Timothy Green Beckley, also known as "Mr. UFO."

Gary Lovisi, whom we interviewed last time, is back with a terrific western story, "Old Aunt Sin." It first appeared in *West Texas War & Other Stories* (Ramble House Books, 2007). Its presentation here benefits from three original illustrations by the multi-talented Michael Neno.

Reviews include current digests like the aforementioned *Betty Fedora* #2, *Paperback Parade* #89, *Fate* #727; a "classic" by Walter B. Gibson, *A Blonde for Murder*, and an invaluable reference by Jeff Canja, *Popular Fiction Periodicals*. We also have a short article on the *Dope Fiends* trading card set, which includes a few digests among all its vintage paperback book covers.

For my own efforts in the realm of fiction, my WIP is a "quadrilogy," a series of four novellas. Each a complete story unto itself with connective threads that weave throughout. Look for the first installment, working title "Invasive Species," in an upcoming *TDE*.

The following retailers stock *TDE* on their shelves along with a wonderful selection of other great reads. Our thanks to Jack, Ron and Mike for your support.

Dark Carnival Bookstore
3086 Claremont Avenue
Berkeley, CA 94705
501-654-7323

Kayo Books
814 Post St.
San Francisco, CA 94109
415-749-0554

Mike Chomko
sites.google.com/site/mikechomko-books/

Until next time, keep up with the world of digest magazines on the Larque Press blog, The Digest Enthusiast pages on Facebook and Pinterest, and with me, Richard Krauss on Goodreads.

Plenty more to come,
-RK

"Just to be on the safe side, lock your door and roll up your window."

Heather Jacobs: Big Fiction

Interview with *Big Fiction*'s editor and publisher conducted by D. Blake Werts

Big Fiction, an independent journal that celebrates the soul of the long story: generous, transportive, and a little wild.

No. 1

No. 2

DBW: Hi Heather, thank you for agreeing to chat with me. We'll start with some basics for our readers and work our way out as we go. You are currently editor/publisher of *Big Fiction* magazine. For a little background, how did you find yourself in this role? What steps got you here?

HJ: Well, as often happens, I think, I created my own position. I founded the magazine, with the hope of providing a venue for longer works. I publish fiction between 7,500 and 20,000 words, which is not what most magazines will do. I've always loved the richness and depth and possibility contained in the long story and novella forms. I wanted to help revive those forms, I guess, and give authors of longer works a satisfying experience by publishing them in an artful format. *Big Fiction* probably wouldn't exist, at least in its current form, without the artistry and willingness of Bremelo Press, who has done all of our letterpressed covers for issues 1–7.

DBW: I'll come back to Bremelo Press in a bit. First I want to dig more into your background. I'm going to go out on a limb here and assume that you didn't come straight to *Big Fiction* without prior experience in publishing/writing? Had you come from another similar position? Were you headed on this path even in school?

HJ: I had vague inklings that I'd like to start a literary journal while I was getting my MFA, but the idea didn't solidify until I was working as an intern with Sarabande Books in Louisville, Kentucky. There I was exposed to the world of indie publishing and instantly fell in love. I discovered, too, that I love editing almost as much—or more, depending on my mood—than writing. At Sarabande, I met Jen Woods, founder of Typecast Publishing and a wonderful letterpress journal called *The Lumberyard*. She was my inspiration; it just sort of clicked for me that I could take an idea and run with it. So that's what I did when I came back to my native Seattle.

I started a family and a literary magazine at the same time. It's been a little crazy. As a writer, too, it was a great way to stay engaged with the literary community, while supporting a form that I love—the novella.

DBW: Was your undergraduate work in literature or some related field? And you continued with the MFA? Were you an avid reader in your youth?

HJ: My undergraduate degree was not in literature, but in anthropology. Which is related, in some ways, because I think the best of fiction is really centrally preoccupied with people, with character. I did go on, after a few intervening years during which I worked as a teacher of English as a Second Language, to get my MFA from the University of Nevada, Las Vegas. I've always been a reader, yes! One of my favorite summer activities when I was a kid used to be lounging on an air mattress in the backyard under the alder trees and reading Erma Bombeck (stolen from my mother's bookshelf, I'm sure). Nowadays I've got three or four books going at once, at least, between pleasure reading, manuscripts, research, etc.

DBW: When were you at Sarabande? And when did you start *Big Fiction* magazine?

HJ: I worked at Sarabande as an intern, and then they were kind enough to employ me off and on as a contest reader and for some editorial consulting, all between 2008 and 2010. I was living in Louisville at the time for my husband's job, and then we moved back to Seattle in 2010. Also in 2010, I had a baby, but I'd already started doing some of the groundwork for *Big Fiction*, and was able to launch the first issue in the fall of 2011, when my son was just about a year old.

DBW: Prior to *Big Fiction*, did you have any favorite digests or periodicals you'd keep around that has influenced what you are producing today? I guess I should ask the question in the present tense as well—maybe you are still picking up new issues of these periodicals today?

HJ: I tend to rotate my subscriptions to magazines, and I am guilty of the same thing I complain about occasionally—the lack of support for print magazines. But, that said, there are many that I enjoy, albeit somewhat randomly over the years. *Bateau*, *Tin House*, *The Lumberyard* (which I mentioned), *The Sun*, *Parcel*, *Pacifica Literary Review*, *Draft*, and *Isthmus* are a few that are currently on my shelf. I also really like *The Southern Review*—I've always been a big fan of their fiction selections.

DBW: Yeah, I think we *all* wish there were more subscribers for these periodicals! I've enjoyed an occasional issue of *Tin House* over the years. Surprised to not see *Glimmer Train* in your list but I suppose there are too many to choose from—we can't catch them all. What do you look for in a literary periodical today? Do any of these have traits you strive to replicate in *Big Fiction*?

HJ: I have enjoyed *Glimmer Train* in years past. I just haven't picked it up recently for some reason, but I should! I should also mention *The Seattle Review*, which is on my shelf right now. A few years ago they announced that they would be solely committed to long-form work—poetry and essay as well as fiction. I think it's a great mission. An author I published in *Big Fiction*, Benjamin Reed, was also published by *The Seattle Review*. I think it's so important to have these outlets for longer, more complex work.

What I look for in periodicals is really the same thing I strive for in *Big Fiction*. I enjoy the physical book, the tactile experience involved in reading, so I really appreciate when a magazine is designed well, inside and out. The work has to be compelling, too. I admit I do like the highly selective periodicals; I appreciate journals that don't try to cram too much in. A slender issue is fine with me. I want to be able to read the whole thing in more or less a sitting or two; I want to absorb the different voices contained therein, and hopefully one or two of them will stand out and surprise the hell out of me. Speaking about fiction, mainly, I don't like to read the same thing over and over—themes and even styles seem to cycle through, fall in and out of vogue, and I kind of hate that. I just want to read a moving, compelling, linguistically interesting story that I haven't read before, or at least not quite in the way the writer has presented it.

DBW: Maybe you can elaborate on what you strive for in each issue of *Big Fiction* magazine?

HJ: Besides having a cool design, these are the same qualities I look for when I'm reading submissions, or, frankly, when I pick up a book in the bookstore and read the first paragraph to see if I want to buy it: It has to resonate, it has to speak to me in a way I haven't been spoken to before, it has to tell me some truth about the world, or expose an old truth in a new way. This is usually done through the writer's attitude to his or her work, through the medium of language. I'm generally not swayed by pyrotechnics, by language for its own sake, but when a unique style is combined with an entertaining story that demands that kind of style, I'll often be won over. An example of this is Alan Sincic's "The

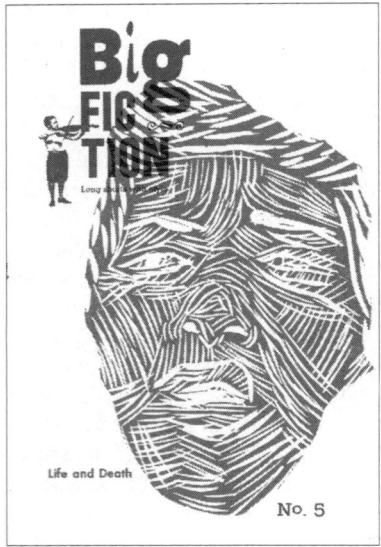

Babe" from Issue 6. Or the naturalistic but rich realism and sense of history I get from a writer like Steve Yates in his novella "Sandy and Wayne" (Issue 4). Or the erudition and tantalizing mystery operating under everything Mylène Dressler writes, as in "The Wedding of Anna F." in Issue 3. Almost every story I've published has been a favorite—I could go on and on—but that's because in order to publish something I have to fall in love with it. And there's no explaining that, really. I do tend to work back and forth quite a bit with authors to polish the work, so I have to be able to read it three, four, five times. I think this leads me to appreciate the language itself a lot more, and also draws me towards characters that are palpable and sympathetic and memorable. In short, stories with many layers that stand up to multiple readings.

DBW: Well having "binge read" six issues of *Big Fiction* in preparation for this interview, I can tell you that you are certainly hitting these marks thus far. I like that each story has this voice that captivates with the very first sentences. And like you've mentioned, that quality is so strong in a well written piece of fiction. To me it is like that meditation/mindfulness state we strive to reach and great fiction can transport you there immediately. Kudos for that!

HJ: Well, thank you for your kind words and appreciation for the writing between the covers of *Big Fiction*. The authors work very hard on these pieces—sometimes for years—and I feel that to recognize that kind of effort and commitment is really necessary. With every single work I've published, I've been thrilled to be part of the process of bringing these stories to an audience. I'm just so grateful for all the wonderful writing that folks have contributed over the past four years. So, kudos to all the *Big Fiction* authors, past and present!

DBW: You've hinted at some aspects of your "production" and our readers are certainly interested in learning more about how these periodicals are put together. You're working hard to find favorites to publish. I'm wondering how many submissions you've been averaging for each issue? I've read that *Glimmer Train* claims to get "40,000 submissions per year" which just seems like madness to me. Are you receiving this kind of volume? And are you reading straight from the submission pile or will they go through other readers first?

HJ: We have two types of submission processes—one, "regular submissions," for lack of a better term, and the other, the annual novella contest, the Knickerbocker Prize. For the contest, I do use readers, but for the non-fee, non-contest submissions, I read most of them myself (with some volunteer help, which I greatly appreciate). I'd say I get a healthy volume of submissions, but not anywhere near what more established magazines get. For one thing, the novella is still a somewhat specialized and unpopular form (though it's gaining popularity!), so that probably keeps the submission volume a little lower. Still, I have plenty to read through, and always rejoice when I find those gems that end up getting published in the magazine.

DBW: Instead of shotgunning you with a bunch of small questions about your production process, maybe you can give us a quick run-through on how *Big Fiction* is put together.

HJ: Well, there are many steps to producing the magazine, all of which I pretty much have a direct hand in. The editorial work and the cover art, printing, and binding are distinct steps, so I'll talk about them each in turn:

First, of course, is finding suitable work. My first criterion, as I've mentioned, is that a piece has to move me, and it has to stand out as having qualities that are "original," in language that surprises me. Then, as much as I can, when I'm not running the contest, I try to find three or four novellas that work together in some thematic way. This doesn't have to be obvious, and I don't put out calls for themed issues, but I do want the several pieces in any given issue to speak to each other, even if only I am explicitly aware of it. (Readers will be aware of it, too, consciously or not.) Then, once I know what I want, I generally work

No. 6

with the authors back and forth for a while—sometimes a few weeks, sometimes a few months—to polish their work. Even highly polished writing, I find, needs ("needs," in my humble opinion!) some editorial tweaking, although I wouldn't take a piece if it needed so much work that I risked messing with the author's intentions or style. I am very light in my editorial touch, but I do think that it takes an outside eye—even if a story has been through a writer's critique group, etc.—before it's ready. I guess I take an old fashioned approach in that regard, since we all hear about "editors who don't edit anymore," but I think that mostly applies to big presses. I have had great experiences with journal editors who have offered suggestions, and I wanted to pass along the same care to authors who come my way. I personally absolutely want someone to edit my work before it goes to print, and in 99% of cases, writers are thrilled that their work is getting that kind of attention.

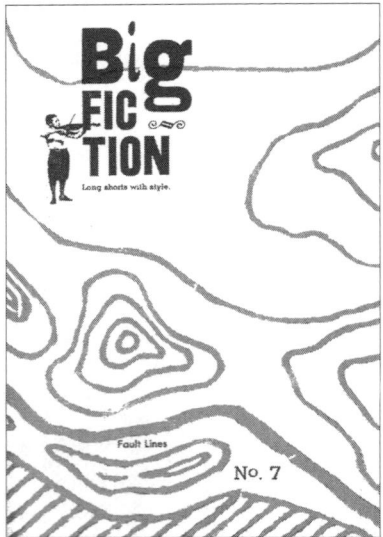

check. All of our covers have been done with original artwork, either linoleum cuts, or hand- or laser-cut wood. The cover layout and text design is all done by Lynda, by hand!

After the cover is under way, I usually get the "guts" printed and try to have that ready at the same time as the covers, then it all goes to the binder, and voila! A book!

DBW: Thanks for walking us through that process. I'm going to admit that I am bonkers over the letterpress work that Lynda and the artists are doing. For me, the "love and care" that goes into the production of *Big Fiction*, as exemplified by the covers and the bookmarks, moves each issue from being a "literary periodical" into the realm of "fine private press." This is not ephemeral material, these are meant to be saved and placed on the prominent sections of a bookshelf. Right beside the classics, even! But maybe that's just me . . . .

I've noticed in the latest issue there is a mention of Dock Street Press that I've not seen before. Are there some changes on the horizon?

HJ: Yes. I'm thrilled that Dock Street Press, a new independent publisher on the Seattle lit scene, is going to take over publication of *Big Fiction*. Dock Street is a young press, founded by editor Dane Bahr in 2012, and they are doing amazing work. Their first book, *The Lucky Body*, by Kyle Coma-Thompson, has garnered some attention, as the title story was selected for *The Best American Short Stories* series. Another book, *Doll Palace* by Sara Lippmann, was nominated for an LA Times Book Award. So they're doing great work and we're really proud to be associated with them.

I don't know if your readers want to hear about layout, but here it is: I had a great designer, DoubleM-Ranch Design, do the original layout for the interior text of *Big Fiction*. I still follow their design, though I actually do the layout myself (cutting and pasting) in InDesign. Lots of proofreading, etc., etc. I have had some excellent volunteer proofreaders over the years, and I thank you all—you know who you are!

The cover art and design is one of my favorite aspects of producing *Big Fiction*. There isn't a submission process for the artwork like there is for the writing. I need to work with people locally, so I just work with who I know. My letterpress printer, Lynda Sherman, at Bremelo Press, has connections with a lot of wonderful artists who understand the printing process, and that's really important. I usually meet with the printer and artist a couple of times—once to get some basic directions for the design, and again to choose colors and do a press

Being two independent publishers in the same town (the same neighborhood, even!), Dane and I decided it made sense to join forces. We're still in discussion about how *Big Fiction* will change (or not) when it becomes an offshoot of Dock Street. Some ideas we've thrown out: Keep the letterpress, or at least elements of it; go to a single author per issue format; include interviews; make each issue unique in terms of the format/look; go to quarterly rather than biannual. These are just our thoughts at the moment. We're taking our time with it.

DBW: Sounds like there could be quite a few changes coming. Not sure I'm comfortable with the single author per issue idea but could really get into the McSweeney's style of changing the format and look with each issue. That's always fun and gives you the opportunity to let the contents dictate the "body" they'd like to live in for a while. I suppose the most important thing is to keep the great fiction coming. You can promise us that much in the near future, right?

HJ: Of course I'd like to keep publishing excellent works of long fiction, and finding the best way to do that is our present challenge. Going to a single-author issue would make *Big Fiction* cheaper and more accessible to more people, which I think is a good thing. And we could probably go to a quarterly publication, keeping the magazine fresher in people's minds. At the moment, these are just ideas, though, and I'm waiting to see what Dock Street and I are inspired to do with it.

Visit *Big Fiction* at:
bigfictionmagazine.com

Visit Dock Street Press at:
dockstreetpress.com

Pulp Fiction Reviews
By Ron Fortier

Weasels Ripped My Flesh!
Edited by Robert Deis with Josh Alan Friedman and Wyatt Doyle
New Texture, 416 pages

Telling you this book is amazing would be perpetuating the biggest understatement of all time. It is a fantastic collection of over-the-top fiction and articles from those garish, exploitive men's adventure magazines that proliferated throughout the '50s, '60s and ultimately died in the 1970s. Chief Editor Robert Deis gives the reader a brief history of this macho movement, connecting it with the post World War II era wherein millions of American veterans came home after having saved the world from the dictatorial evil of fascisms. They returned home heroes not afraid to challenge whatever the future might throw at them while rebuilding a new, brighter society.

This was the macho nature of the times, particularly in the '50s where a John Wayne attitude pervaded both in literature and on the giant silver screen. So it's no surprise these magazines lauded brave, he-men protagonist willing to take on overwhelming odds,

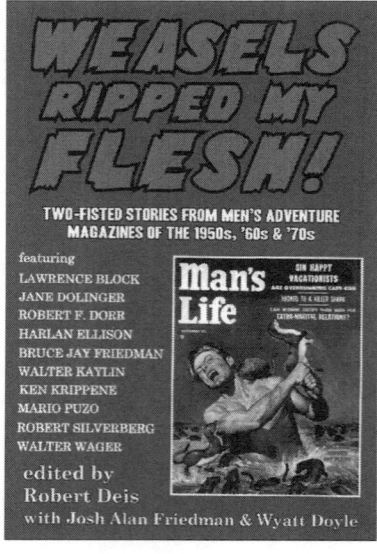

battle ravenous beasts, and take on tribes of love hungry nymphomaniacs. It was the age of the tough guys and dozens of publishers eagerly flooded drugstore racks with their fantastic exploits. Deis makes a solid case that these were the direct descendants of the cheap pulp mags of the '30s and '40s; something he has been extremely passionate about and this collection bears out his theory wonderfully.

What is also startling about

Pulp Fiction Reviews

this anthology is the caliber of writers it showcases; writers who later went on to earn accolades and awards in the more sophisticated, accepted publications of the times. Names like Lawrence Block, Harlan Ellison, Mario Puzo and Robert Silverberg all cut their literary teeth writing for these men's adventure titles, thus making them a training school for the best of the best.

Then there are the bogus scientific articles dealing with drugs and sexual proclivities, never mind the outlandish battles with maddened beasts of all types from the cover spotlighted weasels to ravenous snapping turtles and killer-mad monkeys. *Weasels Ripped My Flesh!* not only entertained the hell out of me, it also educated me in the process. No self-respecting pulp enthusiast should be without this tome. We tip our fedora to Misters Deis, Friedman & Doyle. Thanks for the oh-so enjoyable lesson.

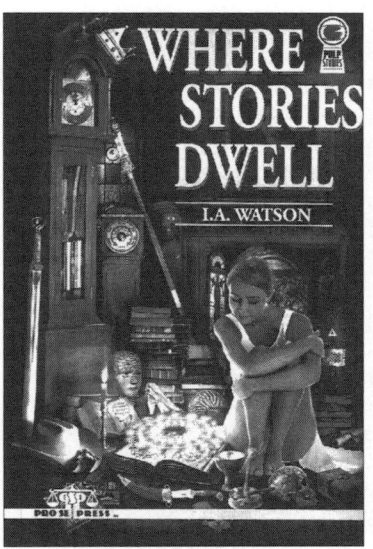

Where Stories Dwell
by I.A. Watson
Pro Se Press, 204 pages

If you haven't been paying close attention over the past few years, then it might have escaped you that one of the leading voices in New Pulp Fiction these days is British writer, I.A. Watson. We can confirm that easily enough by telling you in the past ten years he's won two of the coveted Pulp Factory Awards for Best Short Story. The first was for a Sherlock Holmes story and the second for a frontier adventure featuring the characters from James Fennimore Cooper's *Last of the Mohicans*.

Now that bit of information leads us into this particular volume which is a pure reading delight. You see those Pulp Factory Awards I just mentioned are given out by the internet group on Yahoo called the Pulp Factory; an informal group of New Pulp writers, artists, editors, publishers and fans with a membership numbering 128. Watson has been a member since its inception nearly ten years ago and he has used this particular internet board to regale his fellow members with entertaining essays covering such a wide range of topics it sometimes boggles the mind. Let anyone even hint at an odd tidbit found online and instantly Watson is putting forth a two page dissertation on the subject, filled with insightful commentary, humor and the most outlandish historical notes one could ever imagine.

Watson's Pulp Factory essays have rambled freely over such topics as the birth of heroic fantasy and fairy tales; the legend of King Arthur, heroes, the most powerful female monarch in history, how bad guys die, the purpose of using chapters, the dead World War II hero, Hollywood's misunderstanding of pulps, etc. etc. etc. Just to name a few of the dozens between these pages. There's even an essay explaining the genealogy of British Kings which I confess still confuses me to no end. But what was crystal clear from the first page to the last was just how much fun this book truly is.

And this is where, as a fellow publisher in the New Pulp field, I humbly tip my hat to Tommy Hancock of Pro Se Press. While the rest of us were reading Watson's essays and enjoying them, it was Tommy who had the oh-so brilliant idea of publishing them and producing this remarkable book. Oh, and if you are wise enough to pick up a copy, there's a challenge for you in the very cover by Jeff Hayes, which includes an item related to every single essay in the book itself. Can you pick them all out?

Where Stories Dwell, is that rarest of books; one that both amuses and informs at the same time by a writer I've come to believe is truly the World's Last Renaissance Man. Read it and then tell me I'm wrong. That's a safe bet on my part.

The Man From Mars: Ray Palmer's Amazing Pulp Journey
by Fred Nadis
Tacher/Peguin Books, 263 pages

The first time I ever heard about someone named Ray Palmer, it was in the pages of DC comics Silver Age title, *The Atom*, written by former pulp writer Gardner Fox with art by Gil Kane and edited by Julius Schwartz. What I, and many of my kid colleagues didn't know was that Schwartz had named the minuscule hero after the legendary science fiction pulp editor,

Raymond Arthur Palmer (August 1, 1910 to August 15, 1977), one of the most colorful and controversial characters ever to put pen to paper.

And now we have *The Man From Mars* by Fred Nadis, a truly remarkable, in-depth look at a unique, one-of-kind personality who both helped in the development of science fiction as a legitimate literary genre and was later accused by fanatical fans for having betrayed it by publishing works of sheer fantasy professing outlandish claims.

Crippled by an accident at the age of seven which broke his back, Palmer suffered a botched operation that stunted his growth and left him with a hunchback; he would never grow beyond four feet tall. And yet there was an inimitable will inside him that burned like a spiritual nova propelling him to explore the world's mysteries. Credited with starting the first ever fanzine, *The Comet*, in 1930, Palmer would become a driving force in the sci-fi community until being hired to be the editor of *Amazing Stories* in 1938.

Nadis' narrative is a rollicking, topsy-turvy ride through the ups and downs of one of the most fascinating personages in the cultural history of America. Whether praised or vilified, it was clear Ray Palmer, nicknamed Rap, was an original and this volume is an honest look into both his life and the origins of "geekdom." If you are a fan of the pulps, comic books, science fiction, or occult mysticism, you will find something in this tale to make you sit up and take notice.

I am always leery of biographies, as too many do their subject matter a cruel disservice. The last thing a book about a showman like Ray Palmer should ever be is dull and boring. To Fred Nadis' credit, *The Man From Mars* is truly anything but a fascinating and fun read from beginning to end. Pick up a copy and get to know a truly amazing man. You will be glad you did.

The Executioner: Border Offensive
by Joshua Reynolds (really)
Gold Eagle, 187 pages

We were discharged from the U.S. Army and returned to civilian life upon our return home from Vietnam in the summer of 1968. Sometime shortly after that major life change, we picked up a paperback book from a new publisher called Gold Eagle; the book was *Mack Bolan—The Executioner* and the author was Don Pendleton. It told the story of a Vietnam veteran who comes home to Massachusetts to bury his family, all dead because of the local Mafia which the police cannot bring to justice because of lack of evidence.

Incensed that while he was fighting for his country in a foreign land, his own loved ones were being victimized back home, Bolan realizes he's been fighting the wrong war. He goes AWOL, arms himself and retaliates against the local mobsters responsible for killing his family. By the book's end he is a fugitive on the run but oddly content with his new role; that of an avenging angel who will take on the mob with no regards to his own safety. He will become their Executioner and do what the law cannot; mete out justice.

It was heady stuff but even to a twenty-one-year-old reader, it was also very familiar. Having learned about pulp fiction and their history over the years, it was all too easy to recognize this new paperback series was in fact a brand new attempt at mass market pulp fiction and in his own way, Mack Bolan, had become the Shadow of our times. Confirmation of that theory quickly followed when Gold Eagle not only began issuing new Bolan adventures monthly but also debuted another series about a secret agent trained in martial arts called The Destroyer by Warren Murphy and Richard Sapir. Just like that these two ongoing action packed series launched an entirely new version of American paperback pulps that would flourish throughout the 1970s. Within months other paperback companies were putting forth their own wild and wooly series from the Black Samurai, to the Lone Wolf, the Chameleon and the Baroness to name only a very few. By the end of that decade there were dozens of these on bookstore racks.

Of course Pendleton, being only human after all, couldn't possibly keep churning out book after book after book. Thus the editors of Gold Eagle adopted another practice of the old pulps; they hired ghost writers to produce books all under Pendleton's name. As this became the norm, even after his death, the true author was given their due credit on the indicia page with the phrase, "Special thanks and acknowledgement to John Smith for his contributions to this work." Over the past forty years dozens of authors have found their name in this sentence. Which brings us to this latest Executioner adventure and its author, new pulp writer Joshua Reynolds.

Being familiar with Reynolds' work on reviving classic pulp characters ala Jim Anthony Super Detective and Dan Fowler G-Man, we decided it was time to revisit Mack Bolan after almost twenty years and see if anything had changed in the set formula of the books. Happily the tried and true elements were still there; tons of violent action with a stalwart hero who perseveres despite all manner of physical duress. Reynolds easily slips on the Executioner styling opening the book with Bolan in Mexico having just destroyed a drug cartel's money-making poppy fields. On his way back to the states, he runs afoul of a group of Texas coyotes; men who smuggle illegal Mexican immigrants across the border for cash. Knowing these characters to be merciless thugs, Bolan opts to investigate the situation and inadvertently interferes with an undercover border agent's plan to bring down the two sadistic brothers running the operation.

Then Bolan and his new ally discover the coyotes are working for an al Qaeda agent named Turiq Ibn Tumart who plans on infiltrating the ranks of the poor Mexican workers with one hundred al Qaeda terrorists and in this manner smuggle them into the U.S. to wreak whatever murder and destruction they can perpetrate on unsuspecting American cities. Now it's up to Bolan and the young agent to find a way to stop this deadly convoy and destroy both the coyotes and their fanatical Jidahist allies.

The Executioner—Border Offensive, is an excellent addition to this long-running series and kudos to Reynolds for this gritty, fast-paced new chapter in the ongoing war against evil by the one and only Mack Bolan. Pick it up, pulp fans, you won't be disappointed.

For addtional reviews by Ron Fortier visit his blog: pulpfictionreviews.blogspot.com

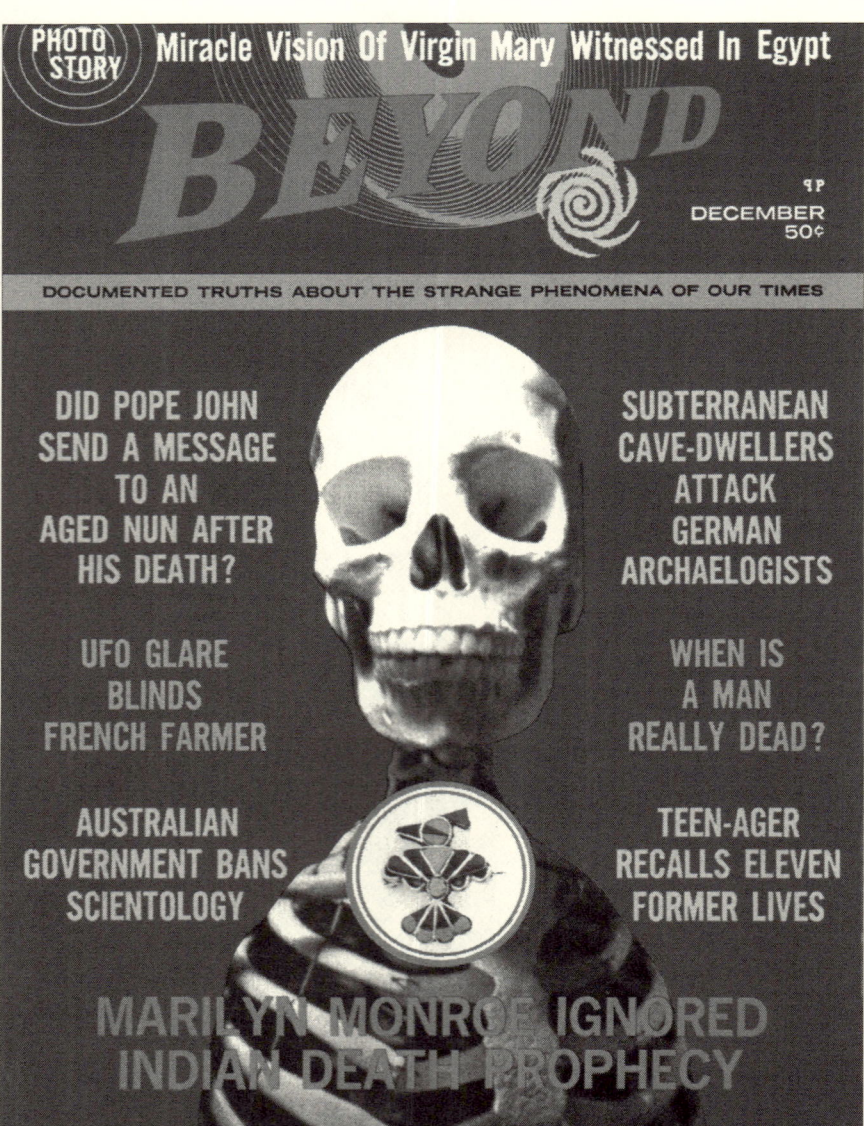

Beyond #4 December 1968

Beyond the Borderline
Article by Tom Brinkmann

The digest *Beyond: Documented Truth About the Strange Phenomena of Our Times* was more Fortean in its concerns than *Borderline* and, quite frankly, it was an inferior imitation of *Fate*. *Beyond* was published monthly by Beyond, Inc., 3 Kuhl Avenue, Hicksville, New York. It was 132 printed pages and cost fifty cents. *Beyond* was digest-sized from September 1968–August 1969 (12 issues) and became an 8.5" x 11" magazine with its September 1969 issue. *Beyond*'s volume number changed each year but, the issue numbers were consecutive or, "whole numbers."

Beyond's publisher was Bernard S. Adelman and its Executive Editor, for the first issue only, was Martin Kessler. Keith Ayling then became the Executive Editor in the second issue (October 1968) and wrote an article for each issue as well as editing them. But, one of the better known Contributing Editors was the prolific paperback author Brad Steiger who wrote a monthly column titled, "*Beyond's* World of the Weird."

In the premier issue's editorial, titled "Welcome to the world of BEYOND," publisher Adelman explained, "I am a busy and successful publisher in fields unrelated to this one, content not to look for new worlds to conquer . . . or at least, so I thought." And, then made this curious statement, "But, fate can shape strange destinies!"

Apparently, the hand of "fate" struck him upside his noggin while on Christmas vacation in Florida. Adelman continued:

" . . . searching for reading material in this area, it hit me suddenly, that there was a desperate need for a magazine in this field. One that would attempt to report all up-to-the-minute psychic events as they happen today, and as they may take place tomorrow, rather than the usual re-hash of old stories which appear repeatedly in numerous unimaginative publications. Suddenly, 'quick like a bunny', the title BEYOND came to mind. It said in one word, the exact direction in which this magazine should be aimed. Suddenly, I knew that I must do this publication! It was as if some strange compelling force [maybe *Fate*] was steering me to the path of BEYOND."

It is total speculation on my part but, might Adelman have been perusing a newsstand for vacation reading material and come across a copy of *Fate* magazine? Was his use of the word "fate" conscious or subconscious? Was the digest-size of the first year of *Beyond* in imitation of *Fate* magazine? Maybe it was just fate, only Adelman's hairdresser knew for sure, or maybe the Shadow! Adelman concludes his editorial by claiming reviewers' response to a "limited printing 'pilot' issue" was "overwhelming."

In October 1967 Roger Patterson and Bob Gimlin packed up some horses and made their way into the California wilderness near Eu-

Beyond premiered in September 1968

reka. The two had packed both still cameras and a 16mm Kodak movie camera for the trek. They followed a creek bed into the forest. Not long into their journey their horses reared up and threw them off. Then, they noticed why—a hairy, apparently female, creature was walking upright on its two legs crossing the creek approximately one hundred feet ahead! Patterson grabbed his 16mm camera and started filming it. What they captured on film, according to the title of Ivan T. Sanderson's cover article on the February 1968 issue of *Argosy* magazine, were the "First Photos of Bigfoot, California's Legendary 'Abominable Snowman.'" *Argosy* used five still frames from the film on their cover (the inspiration for R. Crumb's classic "Whiteman Meets Bigfoot" strip in 1970).

The premier issue of *Beyond*, dated September 1968, had the "Abominable Snowman" as the fringe-science covergirl and also used two stills from Patterson's film but, reversed them. The cover blurb read "Is California's Abominable Snowman A Creature From Another World?" which was the title of the inside article by Franklin Stevens. Adelman's "re-hash" factor was reduced, slightly, by the added theory that the "Abominable Snowman," aka Sasquatch, aka Bigfoot, aka Yeti, might have come from outer space or the inner earth. The other cover blurbs though, were a sure hook for weirdos like myself; how could you resist articles like: "World Powers Hide Super-Baby Race;" "The Man With A Radar Mind;" "U.F.O. Aliens Probe Woman's Mind;" and "Scientists Mystified! Woman Burnt To Ashes By Unknown Force."

Beyond's second issue (October 1968) had a photo of author Raymond Buckland and his wife Rosemary/Rowen on its cover, seemingly nude, and posed as if in a pagan ritual. Given the fact that *Beyond* was published in Hicksville, New York, a Long Island suburb, approximately 30 miles east of Manhattan, there were many articles in *Beyond's* nineteen issues that were by writers who lived in the greater New York metropolitan area. There were also articles about places and/or phenomena that took place there, such as, the issue's "I Live With A Witch" by Buckland in the "Special Bonus Witchcraft Section."

Buckland and his wife lived in Brentwood, another Long Island town, and headed a witchcraft coven and had started a "Witchcraft Museum" in the basement of their home which was by appointment only. Buckland then moved the museum into an old house on a side street off of Main Street (aka Montauk Highway) in Bay Shore, a neighboring town south of Brentwood. As a personal anecdote, my Aunt and Uncle, and three cousins, lived in Bay Shore at that time in the late 1960s. My parents and I would visit Long Island from New Hampshire at least once a year, as all of my mother's family was located there. I don't remember how I heard about it but, on one visit, one of my cousins and I decided to visit the Witchcraft Museum. When we first walked in, there didn't appear to be anyone there; the place was filled with ceremonial daggers and paraphernalia, swords, several animal skulls and skeletons, photos, artwork, and so on. After ogling the contents of the museum for a minute or so, a man appeared at the top of some stairs. He was an older gentleman with whitening hair and a goatee; he asked if we had any questions, and that he would be happy to answer them if we did. Of course, we didn't, because we really didn't know anything about what we were looking at and, I guess, we didn't want to seem stupid. I assume the man was Mr. Buckland. This would have been '68 or '69 and, subject to my foggy memory, as I would have been 13 or 14. A year or so later, I joined the Occult Book Club and would acquire many books on witchcraft, magic, and the supernatural.

Buckland starts his article by going over a shopping list, with his wife Rosemary of items needed for the evening's coven: candles, incense, and charcoal briquets. Then, he continues explaining the polytheistic beliefs of a modern, suburban, witchcraft coven. Rosemary, being the High Priestess and Queen of Witches known as Rowen, is shown in two photos, one nude as the High Priestess and one clothed next to her

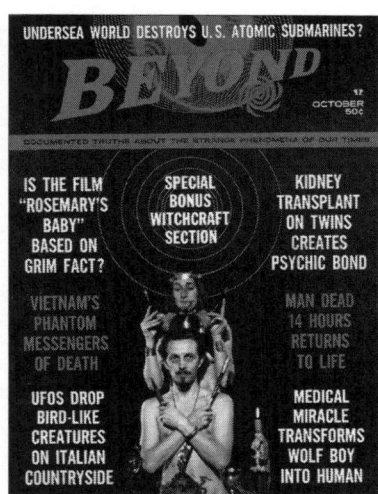

Beyond #2 October 1968

flower and herb garden. Buckland likens his own part in the coven to an altar boy, except during the dark months of winter when he dons the horned helmet and becomes a representation of the Horned God. Buckland also explains that his wife is not an old hag and that the members of the coven do not arrive on broomsticks, but by cars, bus, and train. It sounds very ho-hum for 2015 but, I guess in 1968 it was edgy and hip.

Beyond's second issue also had the cover blurbs, "Kidney Transplant On Twins Creates Psychic Bond;" "Vietnam's Phantom Messengers of Death;" "UFOs Drop Bird-Like Creatures On Italian Countryside;" "Man Dead 14 Hours Returns To Life;" and "Medical Miracle Transforms Wolf Boy Into Human." But, the blurb I found of most interest was "Is the Film *Rosemary's Baby* Based on Grim Fact?" This is the only article, that I know of, which had addressed that premise but, unfortunately, the article didn't deliver with its stories, which were most likely fictitious. I share my birthday with Rosemary's baby, June 28th, although, in the film, and Ira Levin's novel, Rosemary gave birth in 1966, my eleventh birthday.

The full title of the article was, "Steve Devlin Asks: Is This Gripping Movie Based On Fact?," with the subtitle, "Study of Paramount's Film Fantasy, *Rosemary's Baby* Suggests Horrifying Reality," and *Beyond* kicked it off with four stills from the movie, two which were of Rosemary Woodhouse (Mia Farrow) holding a butcher knife in the movie's climactic scene in which she sees her baby for the first time. The other two stills, sandwiched between those of Rosemary, were of her husband, Guy Woodhouse (John Cassavetes) and her obstetrician, Dr. Sapirstein (Ralph Bellamy). In the article's text, the question was posed, "CAN WE DISMISS THE SUBJECT of *Rosemary's Baby* as just a gimmick for a first-class horror movie?" The question was later answered with, "NOT AFTER YOU READ two obscure accounts, ignored by the newspapers of the world, which BEYOND investigated recently—accounts of two women who underwent the most horrible experience a woman can undergo." The article then gave a short synopsis of *Rosemary's Baby* before relating the "terrifying experiences of Maria Fuentes, of Oaxaca, Mexico, and Norah Kovecs, of Szombathely, Hungary."

According to the article, nineteen-year-old Maria Fuentes was in an asylum for the criminally insane for killing her newborn baby. A "*Beyond* correspondent" noticed a few lines about the case in a Mexican newspaper. The supposed correspondent somehow managed to get into the hospital to interview Maria who, "appeared still sane, but just barely" as she related her story of impregnation. Maria had lived with her poor, widowed mother. When her mother died, Maria had no choice but to accept the offer of Madre Tico, a neighboring old woman, "reputed to [be] a witch," who Maria had "felt a strange dislike of." Madre Tico would sit by Maria's bedside singing, incanting, burning strange herbs, and doing other witch-like things. This all created nightmarish dreams for Maria and a sense that her body was not her own. Then, Maria was introduced to Madre Tico's nephew, "Pepe," and thus her impregnation with evil was close at hand.

Beyond claimed that it had "bribed a Communist official" to obtain the court records of sixteen-year-old Norah Kovecs who had abandoned her newborn baby at the foot of a church altar, the infant dying not long after. This, after she noticed it had been born with "two bony appendages growing out of its skull, and one from the base of its spine." Norah told a tale of accepting a ride from a young, "handsome" stranger on her way to school and ending up in an "ancient ruined castle" at a Satanic ceremony where she was impregnated by "the Prince of Darkness."

The key to understanding the film, *Rosemary's Baby*, for me, is in the short speech given by Roman Castevet (Sidney Blackmer) at the end of the film, to Rosemary, about the purpose that her baby: "Adrian," is supposed to fulfill, in other words, the reason why he was conceived, which I quote from the book: "Satan is His Father, who came up from

Hell and begat a Son of mortal woman! To avenge the iniquities visited by the God worshipers upon His never-doubting followers!... . He shall overthrow the mighty and lay waste their temples! He shall redeem the despised and wreak vengeance in the name of the burned and the tortured!"

Besides a wacky article in the *National Examiner* (v6 #49, February 2, 1970) that had the front cover blurb and headline that read, "Girl's Bizarre Confession Links Slaying With 'Rosemary's Baby' - Hippie Cult Killed Sharon Tate To Prevent Birth of 'Satan's Child,'" I've never heard of another story linking the film to reality, until I found this *Beyond* article. I think that the premise is of interest but, the reality would be a lot more mundane than that in the film and these two stories and therefore a lot weirder. All I can say is, Rosemary's baby = YANKEE ROSE.

A photo of Jackie Kennedy was used on the cover of *Beyond's* third issue, dated November 1968, along with the blurb, "Did the Ghost of J.F.K. Communicate With Jackie When She Predicted Bobby Kennedy's Assassination Three Weeks Before It Happened?" Along with Jackie's psychic abilities, the other articles touted on the cover were, "Interviews with the Dead by Psychic Computer," "New World Menace: Mind Control From Outer Space," and "Walking Monster Catfish Attack Florida Wildlife."

Inside the third issue, you would find the first article, "UFOs Use Electric High-Tension Lines for Re-Charging" by Timothy Green Beckley. This was the first of six articles that he published in *Beyond*.

Beyond #3 November 1968

Beckley, the man in blue, "Mr. UFO," is a noted UFOlogist, writer, publisher, editor, radio personality, videographer, and podcaster (see my article about Tim on page 106). Concerning *Beyond*, Tim says, "I never met the publisher of *Beyond*. They were on Long Island. I remember I had to wait forever to get paid. Most of the magazine was crap; half the stories made up. They did have a capable editor [Keith Ayling]."

The fourth issue of *Beyond* (December 1968) had a great cover depicting a skull and rib cage with a small circular inset of an Indian amulet to illustrate the feature "Marilyn Monroe Ignored Indian Death Prophecy" by Fred Grant. There was an incredulous "Editor's Note" that kicked off Brad Steiger's "*Beyond's* World of the Weird" feature that read: "On learning of the Virgin Mary having been seen in Egypt, '*Beyond*' dispatched its Cairo correspondent to investigate. A full report of the phenomenon with pictures appears on page 83."

Beyond Vol. 2 #5 January 1969

Beyond Vol. 2 #6 February 1969

Also, in the pages of the fourth issue, a *Beyond* newsletter was announced: "*Beyond* Magazine Introduces An Important New Publication *Borderline Reports* A Weekly News Letter." The title blows me away! Was Adelman swiping the title of the earlier *Borderline* digest? [See Tom's article "The Borderline Beyond" in *TDE*2.] The ad copy went on to say:

"Compiled Through The Cooperation Of Over 300 LEADING NEWSMEN AND SCIENTISTS Dedicated To Informing The Public About THE PHENOMENA OF OUR TIMES"

In the two-page ad for *Borderline Reports* there were other fantastical claims made such as "BEYOND magazine penetrates the fortresses of silence," and "The true facts will no longer be surpressed!"

"Violence In America Linked To Cult of Assassins" was the main cover blurb for *Beyond*'s January 1969 issue (volume 2 #5) and was illustrated with a painting of Kali, the Hindu goddess of destruction, which was flanked by circular inset photos of Martin Luther King, Jr. and Robert F. Kennedy on one side and Lee Harvey Oswald and John F. Kennedy on the other side. The corresponding feature on the inside had a longer title, "Is Ancient Cult of Assassins Causing Worldwide Violence? Worship of Kali Hindu Goddess of Evil Revived In Europe - Cult Linked To U.S. Assassinations." Maybe the author, Harvey Drew, had just watched The Beatles' movie, *Help!* (1965). But, there is no doubt that 1968 was a politically violent year in the U.S. and Europe; and the article presaged the Tate/LaBianca murders later in August 1969.

Timothy Green Beckley was one of the issue's contributors with his article, "Flying Saucers Project Miraculous Healing Powers." Other notable features in the issue included: "Predictions For 1969 By Famous American Seers" by Brad Steiger, none of which seemed to come true, and "Plenty of Ghosts

Beyond Vol. 2 #7 March 1969

Beyond Vol. 2 #8 April 1969

Inhabit New York City" by paperback author Hans Holzer.

"Facts Indicate Astronauts 'Brainwashed' By Unknown Forces From Outer Space" announced the cover of the February 1969 (v2 #6) issue which used a photo of the crew of Apollo 7. The corresponding article by Harvey Drew added the opening blurb "Rebellious Behavior Patterns of Apollo 7 Crew Suggests Extra-Terrestrial Hostility - Soviet Cosmonauts Report Similar Experiences." The cover also had one of *Beyond's* best blurbs ever, "Bob Kennedy's Face Appears On Coal Shovel," as well as, "UFO's Paralyze Latin America" and "Do Animals Have E.S.P.?"

"Primitive Cult Practices Psychic Cannibalism" and "A Man Who Sees Without Eyes" were two articles mentioned on *Beyond's* cover of March 1969 (v2 #7). And, once again, a still from Roger Patterson's Bigfoot film was used. In fact, it was one of the same stills used on the cover of the first issue but, this time turned into black and white. "Five More 'Abominable Snowmen' Sighted By Scientist In Nepal Mountains" the cover claimed while underneath the photo were six triangular, commemorative postage stamps from Bhutan with an artist's depiction of the Abominable Snowman from different sightings. Adelman would later "re-hash" the Patterson photos for a third time on the cover of *Beyond's* first 8.5" x 11" inch issue (September 1969).

A detail from the "Hell" portion of Heironymous Bosch's "Triptych of the Garden of Earthly Delights" painting was used as the cover of the April 1969 (v2 #8) issue, in connection to the article "Is N.Y. Artist John Graham A Reincarnated Heironymus Bosch?" by Tamara Franklin. John D. Graham (1886–1961) was born Ivan Gratianovitch Dombrowsky in Kiev, Ukraine and came to America in 1920. He had a great influence on the New York School of painting which included Willem de Kooning for whom

Beyond Vol. 2 #9 May 1969

Graham was a mentor. Graham was allied to Surrealism and Cubism and his book *System and Dialectics of Art* (1937) helped to define the Abstract Expressionism of the 1940s. Later in his life, Graham's paintings leaned more towards Realism. After Graham's fifth wife died he met, and fell in love with, Ultra Violet, the Warhol superstar. The article gives facts about both Bosch and Graham's lives but, also admits little is known about either. The piece is mostly speculation surrounding both artists' occult beliefs and possible drug use, although I see no similarity between their paintings. There was an exhibition of John Graham's work at the Museum of Modern Art in 1968 which inspired the feature in *Beyond*.

"Man Lives 256 Years On Oriental Herbs" and "Tarot Cards Predict Death of An Adulteress" were the two main articles featured on the cover of the May 1969 (v2 #9) issue. The issue also contained Tim Beckley's third article for *Beyond*, "Red-Eyed, Winged Creature Terrorizes West Virginia Town," which had to do with the Mothman, which I go into in my article on Tim (page 106).

"Will Liz Taylor Be Destroyed By the Deadly Curse of the Krupp Diamonds [sic]?" asked the main cover blurb of *Beyond's* June 1969 issue (v2 #10) which had "Liz" on its cover. Other blurbs included "Reincarnation—Fact Or Fantasy?" and "Dying Woman's Soul Transplanted Into Sick Girl's Body." But, the issue most notably contained an obscure article by Ed Sanders, lead member of the musical group, The Fugs, who was also proprietor of the Peace Eye Bookstore on New York's Lower East Side in the '60s, and author of *Tales of Beatnik Glory*, *The Family: The Story of Charles Manson's Dune Buggy Attack Battalion*, *Fug You*, and other books and articles. This was Sanders' only article for *Beyond*, which was based on a real case that took place in France in 1968; it was titled, "Children of Sorcerer Vanish Mysteriously—Were they lost to forces from the unknown?"

The "sorcerer" in question was Maurice Gerard (1929–1999), aka "Swami Natkormano," aka "The Mage of Marsal," who was raised on his parents' farm in the northern French town of Marsal. Gerard left home at age 23 and moved to Paris; there, he studied Yoga and the occult. In 1955 Gerard received a "telepathic message" telling him to travel the world to become "initiated into occult knowledge." This he did, visiting Egypt, Iran, India, and Hawaii where Gerard gained oracular powers and also became able to make statues speak, "after educating them." Gerard returned to Paris in 1958 and met a medium, Josiane, at an "occult society." They were attracted to each other by their mutual interest in the occult and were married within the year. In 1964 the two moved back to Gerard's hometown of Marsal. The Gerards opened an Ashram and Maurice took the title of "Swami Natkormano" and Josiane became "High Priestess Alfeola." By that time, the couple had produced five children. On November 25, 1968 two of the children went missing, Gabriel, 6 and Pascal, 3.

That morning, Maurice Gerard showed up at the local Marsal police station, hysterically claiming two of his children had been kidnapped during the night. He explained that he had heard noises coming from his basement, where his "Ashram" was located. On his way to the basement to investigate, he noticed that the door to it had been opened, as well as the front door leading to the street. Hearing "howling" noises from outside, Gerard looked into the night and saw "immense vague shapes moving about," then he heard a shriek.

When the police descended on Gerard's home to find evidence of the kidnapping, their inquiry turned to suspicion when they entered his basement/Ashram, of which there are several photos in the article. They found it festooned with occult symbols, statuary, artwork, and paraphernalia from floor to ceiling. But, there was no sign of the missing children or the kidnappers and, no ransom note. After relating the story of the kidnapping more than once to the police, Gerard then told them that one of his many statues had been stolen two months earlier; this was a wooden statue of the Buddha that

Beyond Vol. 2 #10 June 1969

he had "trained to speak." He then said he thought it to be the work of two German Rosicrucians who had come and asked him for the two children right before the statue had been taken. Gerard further explained he would hypnotize his wife Josiane and the statues would speak through her. With more intense questioning from the police, Gerard went into a "Yoga trance."

The police consulted with Roland Cave, "Yoga expert," who eventually got Gerard to talk to him and explained he had been working with the "Seventh Ray." Cave told the authorities, "'The Seventh Ray' is called the 'Green Ray' or the 'Ray of Death,' because all those who have tried to pierce its secrets are dead." This was enough to make the investigators' strong suspicions that Gerard had a hand in his children's disappearance even stronger. On closer inspection of the missing children's room, the police noticed strange pieces of copper wire protruding from the wall over each of their

Beyond Vol. 2 #11 July 1969

beds; when traced back to their origin, it turned out the wires led down to Gerard's Ashram in the basement. When asked, Gerard explained that his two children had been in "poor health" and claimed the wires "were to carry mystic sources of energy ... and transmit them to the children's bodies during their sleep, inducing health and strength." Then, Gerard went into another trance.

It is not mentioned in Sanders' article, but through a Google search, I discovered an article on Gerard and the case, in French. Loosely translated, it said that Gerard had spent 53 weeks in prison but, was let go for lack of evidence. Maurice Gerard died in April 1999, taking whatever secrets he had, or didn't have, with him.

Bobby Darin was the coverboy for the feature, "Bobby Darin Tells of Mystic Revelation At the Grave of Robert Kennedy," on the July 1969 issue (volume 2, #11). The issue also contained Jaye P. Paro's first article for *Beyond*, titled "Mount Misery—Weird Mystery of L. I.—Uncanny Silence, Strange Noises, History of Murders and Secret Indian Rites Create Sinister Atmosphere." It would take twenty to thirty minutes to drive from Hicksville, Long Island, where *Beyond* was published, to Huntington, where Mt. Misery Road is located; and if you drove south from there, in another fifteen minutes you would reach Farmingdale, where Jaye Paro lived at the time she wrote the article. Paro was a Long Island radio journalist on WBAB, a psychic detective, and an occasional *Beyond* contributor in the later issues. She was also "the contactee 'Jane' in *The Mothman Prophecies* [1975]" written by the Fortean journalist and author, John A. Keel (1930–2009), who was a close friend of Tim Beckley's.

The history of Mount Misery goes back as far as the Indian legends of its being inhabited by evil

The Mothman Prophecies by John Keel

spirits. The area was settled in the late 17th century and it is one of the highest points on Long Island. The geography was created by the glacier which had stopped on the North Shore, turning the land into hills and hollows; the South Shore is flat. The explanations of why it was named Mount Misery are many but, the most accepted and plausible is that of wagons that had to travel over the rough road that led over it would break their wheels if not going slow and carefully. The reasons for the supernatural/paranormal atmosphere surrounding Mount Misery are numerous, lunatic asylums that burned down; teenage suicides; car crashes; ghosts; strange noises; cigar shaped UFOs with weird lights, and so on.

Jaye Paro's interest in the paranormal phenomena of Mount Misery shifted into high gear when she received a call to her radio show by a "sobbing, hysterical" woman who had been renting a house there in the summer of 1966. The caller claimed that one night while she was walking her dog she saw in the middle of the road ahead ". . . two half-naked brown men who looked like Indians in a Western movie." The two men appeared to be fighting when one stabbed the other with what looked like a spear. As the one man lay dead the other let out a shriek and started dancing. At that point, both the woman and her dog, were seemingly paralyzed with shock and fear. Then the two men faded into the night. When Paro arranged to meet the spooked caller, to interview her, she had packed her bags and was ready leave the rented house.

Paro's interest in Mount Misery's paranormal activity increased and

Beyond Vol. 2 #12 August 1969

she spent a lot of time there "haunting it" to experience some of it but, nothing happened. Until, one night Paro awoke and received a message telling her that if she went to Mount Misery she would see something. At 8 a.m. that morning Paro and two friends drove there to see something—and did! Paro had taken several photos that turned out "foggy" but, there was a blurry photo in the article of what Paro and her friends saw, described thusly, "It seemed to be a black mass in human form that moved silently through the tangle of bushes." The article ended with a signed statement by one of Paro's friends saying that on January 12, 1969 he had driven to Mount Misery, with Ms. Paro and saw the thing as described. Paro's trips to Mount Misery had come to a scary end.

As mentioned previously, *Beyond's* August 1969 issue (volume 2 #12) was the last that was digest-sized. "They Were Warned That Death Beckoned!" was the cover feature. The issue contained

Beyond Vol. 2 #13 September 1969, the first magazine-size issue

another article by Tim Beckley titled, "Did Under Sea UFO Destroy French Submarine?" The other articles included, "L.S.D. Is Claimed To Aid Psychic Research," "India's Holy Man Creates Jewels Out of Air," "Secret Photographs of Witchcraft Rituals," and "Will Ancient Curse Destroy New York Museum?" Jaye Paro's second article for *Beyond* was also in the issue titled, "A Miracle At Garabandal."

Beyond ran for seven more issues, that I'm aware of, at the 8.5" x 11" size. Its last was dated March 1970, which stated wrongly that it was v3 #18 on the contents page but was actually the nineteenth issue and had "Ted Kennedy For President" as the cover feature. *Beyond's* February 1970 issue was the "true" eighteenth issue.

Tom Brinkmann writes about unusual, off-the-beaten-path magazines, digests, and tabloids at his website: badmags.com His books *Bad Mags* volumes 1 and 2 are available from amazon.com. Grab one or the pair and you'll be off and running into the land of twilight pulp and the glossy adult hinterland!

Brinkmann started writing reviews of zines and books, and articles on weird magazines for *Headpress Journal* (UK) in 1998. His Bad Mags site has been on the Internet since 2004; *Bad Mags* V1 was published in 2008, followed by *Bad Mags* V2 in 2009. Since then he continues his pursuit of printed matter of unusual interest in his self-published zine *On the Rack*, of which there have been three issues. To get your copies, which are in limited supply, contact him at: vaioduct@aol.com

Dope Fiends Trading Cards
Article by Richard Krauss

"Enter the forbidden world of addicted teenagers, drug-crazed criminals, and wanton women!"

The *Dope Fiends* trading card set provides reproductions of vintage paperback book covers from the 1950s and 1960s. The set of 36 cards was compiled and annotated by Doug Aanes and first printed in 1995 by Kitchen Sink Press.

The set features highly collectable books. Most were published in true paperback book format, but a few debuted in the paperback digest format like N.R. de Mexico's *Marijuana Girl* (Uni Books #19, 1951), which went on to become a poster child of the U.S. House of Representatives' Select Committee on Current Pornographic Materials.

The card images were either captured from pristine copies of the original PBOs or retouched to provide the clean, clear reproductions for the cards.

Aanes provides a useful mix of backstory on the author, the cover artist, the book's historical notoriety and/or back cover copy

clipped from the original editions.

For example, *The Pusher* by Evan Hunter writing as Ed McBain:

"*His sister was on heroin! She sold her body to pay for it. She gave him his first shot as a joke. In a short time, he was on it steady.*"

Here, one of the 87th Precinct's cops struggles with his son's heroin addiction. The author displays obvious concern for the young victims of narcotic addiction, and places the blame on the pushers.

Starting in 1956 Hunter wrote over forty-three 87th Precinct novels, but he's perhaps best known as the author of **The Blackboard Jungle**, a novel of juvenile delinquency in an urban high school, which, in its 1955 movie form, helped propel rock 'n' roll to prominence. The grim scene on Charles Bingers' cover suggests that not only drugs, but auto-eroticism, is involved in the boy's death.

The set includes a full color box with the wide-eyed junkie stripped from the cover *I Was a Drug Addict* (card #21) by Leroy Street in collaboration with David Loth (cover by Julian Paul).

Books featured in the set include *Too Hot for Hell* by Keith Vining (cover by Norman Saunders), *Monkey On My Back* by Wenzell Brown (cover by Owen Kampen), *It Ain't Hay* by David Dodge (cover by Gerald Gregg), *Marihuana* by William Irish (cover by Bill Fleming), *Junkie* by William Lee (cover by Norman Saunders), *Rapture Alley* by Whit Harrison (cover by Rudolph Belarski), *The Golden Spike* by Hal Ellson (cover by Robert Macguire) and dozens more.

Cornell Woolrich wrote *Marihuana* as William Irish. Here's Aanes' description:

Poor King Turner. A reluctant participant in his first marijuana experience, he suddenly becomes a killer and flees into the streets of New York. As the police net closes in, a stoned and panicky Turner kills again. At the end of his path of destruction lies a surprise ending.

Cornell Hopley Woolrich is widely recognized as a master of suspense who created a bleak noir atmosphere in all his books. The "noir" themes often involved ordinary innocent citizens condemned or trapped by a malevolent fate. His own life story is marked by the sort of unhappiness and claustrophobia that permeates his stories. In his early years, he reputedly cruised the waterfront dressed in a sailor's uniform; however, he was ambivalent about his sexuality and kept this part of his life secret.

The *Dope Fiends* trading card set is no longer in print but can be found with relative ease in secondary markets. Don't be confused by another card set with a similar title, *Famous Dope Fiends*, which features portraits of celebrities like David Crosby, Bela Lugosi, Janis Joplin and Judy Garland.

Planetstorm
Science Fiction by Joe Wehrle, Jr.

Danger threatens Rick Mills and Asher Hayes of the Outpost Service when their survey ship lands on an alien world. As they begin their exploration they soon learn that even across the voids of space Mother Nature rules.

The tiny survey ship lay at rest beneath an unfamiliar sun. In the operations cubicle, Rick Mills began the complicated process of sealing himself into the bulky, sand-colored field suit. He double-checked the gear as he loaded it onto the suit and attached the proper input studs. When he installed the heat-pack, it beeped, he winced, and he hurriedly unclipped and reset it properly, hoping his grandfather hadn't noticed the telltale sound.

The gentle snicker from behind told him otherwise. Rick turned a grim face toward the amused one of Asher Hayes.

"Oh, don't take yourself so seriously, boy," the older man said with compassionate humor. "I still hook 'em up wrong now and then, after all these years. Hey, listen, what are we here for, anyway?"

Rick looked surprised and puzzled. "Huh? Well, we . . . we're here to do the first habitation analysis," he stammered. "Uh, to see if the planet can be colonized, or at least utilized for its vegetative or mineral resources."

Asher made a brushing motion in the air. "No, no," he said, shaking his head. "You and I are here to have fun. Let the rest of them up there on the mother ship, light years away from their homes because they want the big credits, let them go around all sad and stony-faced if they want to. We're family. And we'll do a better job if we have a good time doing it. When I found out my sixteen-year-old grandson wanted to join the Outpost Service . . . well, you know I pulled all the strings I could pull, to get them to let us work together. The only surprise to me is why you agreed to team up with an old guy who's neglected you most of your life." Asher grinned again, but his eyes were serious.

Rick was stunned. "I never felt like that, Granfa'r. I wished we could've been together more, sure. But you sent all those vid chips, showing us where you'd been and what you and the rest of the team had discovered, and you always had a personal message for everybody, especially for me. And those chips you sent me for my birthday . . . I played them over and over. Good thing they don't wear out, huh? I guess you were training me for this job before either of us knew I was going to apply for it. And besides . . . You're not old!"

"Well, that part's true enough," Asher said, flexing his arm muscles.

Grandfather and grandson looked at each other with moist eyes, much emotion and some embarrassment about the emotion. Asher cleared his throat.

"So, are we going to stand here and cry on each other's shoulder all afternoon, or what?"

Rick grinned. "We can if you like."

"Out the hatch with you."

The land outside the survey craft was barren and still. Now and then a faint breeze ruffled the spare tufts of orange grasslike vegetation, but that was all. No birds soared overhead, no animal life moved on the ground.

Asher considered. "Okay, we saw the chips of those small, plant-eating creatures that the probe remotes spotted. Let's move off toward the hill there. Those trees—or whatever they are—look like something the probe recorded."

The probes had also verified that the planet's atmosphere seemed perfectly breathable, so Rick and Asher were not wearing helmets. They were wearing dispersion filters which snugly adhered to the lower part of their faces and insured that no wind-blown spores or microscopic insects entered their respiratory systems. Because they were so permeable, the filters worked without distorting their voices, and the bottom section could be lifted to allow for eating or drinking in a sheltered place.

The hill was actually just a rise of land, flattened on top, and the top was closely populated with the trunks of the towering things they'd seen on the probes' recordings. These were yellow-brown and fleshy-looking, and while they had no leaves, they gave the impression of earthly trees because the tops bloomed out wide like terrestrial broccoli. Below the tops, long, loose tendrils seemed to form a connection between trees. Asher tested the surface of one of the trunks cautiously with his gloved hand. He looked at Rick and frowned as it seemed to draw away from his touch.

"Our biological and botanical studies should give us a starting point, but . . ." He shook his head. "Some of the things you run into sure are a puzzle. Makes you feel like the rules don't quite apply."

"I know. Oh! There's one of the animals!"

A dark brown, coarse-furred creature, somewhat like a pig but with a shovel-shaped snout and tiny, deep-set eyes was emerging from a burrow. It was as wide as a man, and probably weighed more. Asher kept a hand near his stun rod, and Rick activated the vid recorder at his belt.

The animal didn't appear to notice them. It shuffled along, scooping the tufts of grass up with its wide mouth and cutting the stuff with rows of small, chisel-like teeth. When the thing came close to one of the "trees," it began scraping its teeth across a ridge in the trunk. The "tree" shuddered and flailed its lower appendages, but they were either too high or too short to reach the gnawing creature, and it ignored the movements. A larger organism nearby, with appendages which nearly reached the ground, swung one of them across its trunk to give the animal a sound buffet on the side of the head. The creature squealed and lurched away with an awkward, humping gait through the alien vegetation.

Rick deactivated the recorder and observed the "trees" in a new light. "Did you see that? The tree couldn't defend itself, so the one beside it jumped in!"

"Sure looked like it."

"Wow!"

"I guess we won't be cutting any specimen samples off these things," Asher said, wryly. "Besides which, if you'll notice, the breeze that seemed like a lot of nothing when we came out of the ship is building up to be some real gust. They make pretty good extrapolations from the probe surveys, but we don't know the whole story about climatic conditions here. So maybe we oughta go back and hole up for a while, 'til we see what's happening."

Rick saw the frantic way the tufts of orange grass were rippling, and heard the weird notes the wind was playing through the limbs and tendrils of the vegetation. The sky was rapidly darkening, too.

"Something's blowing up, all right. Are we going to take any samples now?"

"Oh, I think we should probably take some soil with us, That way we can run some preliminaries on it while we're waiting out this weather. Maybe we can scoop the science brains on the big ship. That would be fun!"

Rick grinned and watched

while his grandfather produced a small specimen pouch and tramped over to where the ground seemed less firmly packed. But as he bent down to scrape up his sample, the ground gave way beneath him. He clawed at the sides of the hole as he fell, but he only succeeded in pulling more dirt down with him.

Rick stood paralyzed for a moment, then he started forward. The rising wind caught him and nearly sent him into the hole with his grandfather, but he braced his legs and fought it. He got down on his knees and cautiously crept to the edge. He could see nothing in the growing darkness and his throat constricted with terror.

"Granfa'r! Are you all right?"

"Nothing broken," Asher's voice called out. "But, listen, Rick. You better come back for me after this windstorm dies down. It's getting worse by the minute. I'll . . . probably be safe enough down here."

"No you won't! The wind's blowing all the loose dirt and stones in the area across here. It must be coming down on you, isn't it?"

"Yes, but . . . Rick, I think we're . . . running out of time!"

A fierce hail of small particles and plant stems rained across the hillside now, clattering against his field suit and equipment casings, stinging his face. Rick rummaged through his side pack. "That hole you're in was probably covered over by a storm just like this one, Granfa'r!"

There was silence from the hole, then Asher replied quietly. "That could be."

Rick dug his infragoggles out and put them on. He couldn't keep his eyes open any longer in the face of this dry torrent. "Listen, I'm sending my all-purpose cable down."

"It's way too short, Rick. It'll just barely reach."

"I know. Couple it to yours."

"Good idea. I wasn't thinking. But what are you attaching it to?"

"This tree trunk here."

"Try it. But be careful it doesn't clobber you. Don't damage the surface."

"Right." He felt a tug as the cables snapped together, then he pulled some of the line back, crawled over to circle the narrow trunk with it, and snapped the end onto one of the side connectors. He tensed as a long tendril lowered itself and played across his back. But nothing else happened.

"Better put your goggles on, Granfa'r. It's pretty bad up here. Can you use the connectors for handholds?"

"Sure! Coming right up!"

In a matter of seconds, Asher's head and shoulders emerged from the hole. Rick reached under the older man's arms and helped to hoist him the rest of the way out. Then they uncoupled the cable.

"This is terrible," Asher shouted to Rick, as he shielded his face with an arm.

"Don't try to stand up! It knocks you right over!"

Asher shook his head sadly. "Half a mile to the ship. And we can't run! We can't even walk! Rick . . . "

"Wait! Something's happening!"

It had suddenly grown even darker. But the wind force had diminished. Rick and his grandfather stood up and looked around them.

The tree-things were bent

forward into a circle around them, broccoli tops folded back flat against the curving trunks to form a protective dome.

"They're shielding us!" Rick exclaimed. "I can't believe it!"

Asher looked up at the makeshift dome and laughed. "Thank you, friends!" he shouted, spreading his arms. He laughed again. "I'm sure they can't understand a word I'm saying, probably don't even understand the concept of language. But maybe they can sense our gratitude." He turned back to Rick. "Of course, you're the one who really saved us."

Rick stared. "Me? How can you say that, Granfa'r?"

Asher shrugged. "We saw that group preservation is a prime motivator with these things. They help each other. And I think when you refused to leave me and save yourself, they saw something they liked. Sensed something, rather, as they don't appear to have eyes.

At least it triggered some protective response that made them close ranks like this. Dogs will save humans, why shouldn't these things, if they're at all empathetic?"

"Well, I couldn't have saved myself anyway. There wasn't nearly enough time, even if I had started back the instant you fell."

"But you didn't know that. And by staying, you saved us both. Now we just wait it out. Did you bring any food along, by chance? I'm suddenly getting very hungry!"

Rick grinned and started rustling through his side pack.

↙ ↓

Joe Wehrle, Jr. is a writer and artist. His stories and artwork have appeared in the *Cauliflower Catnip Pearls of Peril, Menomonee Falls Gazette, 1971 Clarion Anthology, Vampirella, Two-Gun Raconteur, Worlds of If, Galaxy, The Digest Enthusiast* and many other publications.

The Digest Enthusiast book two

Interviews
Gary Lovisi: Paperback Parade
Steve Darnall: Nostalgia Digest
Robert Lopresti: AHMM, EQMM

Articles
Borderline
Astounding Stories Trading Cards
Mysterious Traveler
Mister No
Beyond Fantasy Fiction
Australian Crime Digests
Archie Comics Digests

Reviews
Monster! #15
Shanks on Crime
Pulp Crime Digests Guide
Asimov's July 2015
Big Fiction #7
Dead Weight (Jonathan Press J56)

Paperback Parade #88
Analog #1000

Fiction
"Passenger for the Night Train"
 by Joe Wehrle, Jr.
"Sweet and Sour" by D.D. Ploog
"Painesville" by Richard Krauss
"In the Fight for His Life" by John Kuharik

Illustrations and cartoons
Joe Wehrle, Jr. (cover), Brad Foster,
Andrew Goldfarb, Michael Neno,
D.D. Ploog and Bob Vojtko

Specifications
Nearly 100 cover images
152 pages
Available from amazon.com
$8.99 Print, $2.99 Kindle

A Blonde for Murder by Walter B. Gibson
Review by Richard Krauss

Late in the 1940s, a series of five Atlas Mystery digest paperbacks were launched. Their covers and back covers display the Atlas globe, but inside Vital Publications, Inc. is listed as the publisher. And in the case of *A Blonde for Murder*, the story is copyright Current Detective Stories, Inc., a publishing outfit owned by Martin Goodman.

The second in the short-lived series was *A Blonde for Murder*, written by famed Shadow author, Walter B. Gibson. The story features his magician character Johnny Ardini, who is highlighted as simply "Ardini" in the cover blurb and throughout most of the novel. The artwork, attributed to artist Peter Driben, shows the story's mysterious blonde murder suspect about to be apprehended.

Inside, the 128-page story is summarized on the inside front cover: "Ardini, the famous Magician, was more pleased than surprised when his hand-picked "volunteer" from the audience was replaced by 110 pounds of lovely glamour running across the stage, chased by a bulky figure waving a pistol. Before long his admiration changed to chagrin, and wonder . . . why did fate have to hand him dynamite wrapped up in a package so alluring that he was helpless to stay away? Before he knew it, Ardini was a suspect, spectator, and detective in a case that startled New York; a case involving jewelry thefts, mystery, magic . . . and murder.

"Magic, and a better-than-average power of deduction, were on Ardini's side, though, and soon he was giving some crime-busting lessons to the police. He even had time to take some lessons himself, and he learned a thing or two about romance from a beautiful, 110 pound instructor with plenty to teach."

As fans of Gibson's Shadow novels already know, Gibson was a one of the pulp era's elite authors. I've read over a dozen Shadow novels so I was eager to see how he'd handle a different cast of characters. The copyright on this digest magazine is 1948, so I assume it was written near the end of his remarkable run on the Shadow. Yet, aspects of the writing seem more like something you'd expect from someone with far less experience. The production too seemed a bit rushed, based on the number of typos.

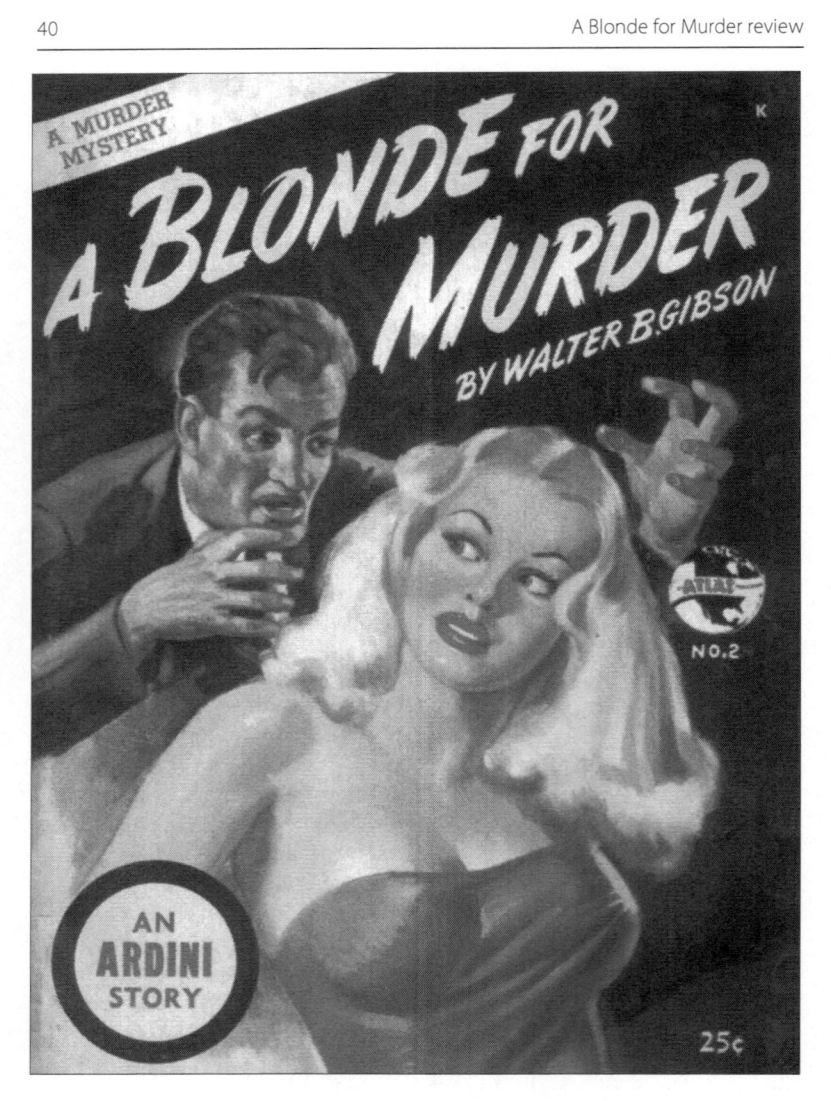

The plot involves an insurance swindle, where a gang steals jewelry from wealthy dupes and works both their victims and the insurance companies from multiple angles. It's a complicated scam and the romance so prominently hyped in the promo is barely even suggested in the novel. Ardini and his supporting cast spend considerable wordage pontificating about the interworking of the jewelry ring in excruciating detail.

Like many crime fighting heroes, Ardini's wits and skillset are far more advanced than the police he assists. Of course, as a magician he's a master of sleight of hand and misdirection, but he can also disguise himself so completely even an acquaintance cannot penetrate his deceptions.

And his photographic memory ". . . raised Ardini's skillful magic to its flawless state, for always he checked the reactions of his audience to every detail of his work, so that he could correct a sleight by changing his hand tilt a fraction of an inch, or could alter his timing on a split second basis."

A Blonde for Murder is one of the lesser Gibson novels. The first two-thirds were a slog, but fortunately picked up considerably in the final third, including the quality of the writing. When the action finally accelerates and the Gibson "magic" materializes on the page, it left me with a higher level of satisfaction than I expected half-way in.

Here's a quip out of left field from the lead Detective on the case, just as things are wrapping up. "Big business guys go bad sometimes and killing people isn't past them, or they wouldn't be coaxing people to ride in airplanes and streamliners and to buy faster automobiles."

I don't know if there were other Ardini stories, but I suspect not. The character certainly had potential and if Gibson had written other adventures it's likely he'd have added more depth and refinements to his hero.

Gibson also wrote the final book in the Atlas Mystery series, *Looks that Kill!* featuring Valdor, a master mind reader. Both novels were available in reprint editions from Fiction House Press (through CreateSpace), but I didn't find them in a recent check of their website—however, they were listed on Amazon. The original Atlas Mystery editions can be found through secondary markets.

↙ ↓

"That knife must be the murder weapon.
Look at all the blood on it."

Super-Science Fiction Vol. 1 #4 **June 1957 cover by Ed Emshwiller**

THE HORROR
OF THE CREEPING TERROR
MONSTERS!!!

Article and overview by Peter Enfantino

"I survived a reading of the complete run of all eighteen issues of *Super-Science Fiction* magazine!!!!"

It was slim pickins' for horror fiction in the late 1950s.

Weird Tales had ceased its seemingly endless run as a digest in 1954, a mere shadow of its former self, which left only Michael Avallone's enjoyable *Tales of the Frightened* (and that stiffed after only two issues) and a handful of horror anthologies (Zacherley's two Ballantine collections immediately come to mind) to satiate those who preferred their fiction supernatural rather than scientific.

On the opposite end of the spectrum, the science fiction movie boom of the mid-1950s, led by *The Day the Earth Stood Still*, *War of the Worlds*, and *The Thing*, helped spur on a proliferation of science fiction digests on the newsstand. You could choose from the venerable *Amazing*, *Astounding*, or *F&SF*; the lighter *Imaginative Tales*, *Imagination*, and *Fantastic* (which featured at least a handful of classic horror stories in the 1950s); or you could sneak a peek over your shoulder and hope no one saw you actually buy the new issue of *Super-Science Fiction*.

The cover of the first issue of *SSF* (published by Headline Publications in Holyoke, Mass.[1]) certainly would not catch the attention of the average horror fan. It featured Kelly Freas' painting of a space-

---

1 Holyoke's history is an article unto itself, it would seem. Under a variety of publishing names such as Headline, Columbia, Pontiac, and Candar, the house produced scads of digests including *Off Beat Detective*, *Sure Fire Detective*, *Web Terror Stories*, *Double Action Western*, *Original Science Fiction*, *Trapped* and *Guilty* (the latter two edited by *SSF*'s W.W. Scott) until its apparent demise in the mid-60s. There's a great behind-the-scenes piece by Harlan Ellison in Gary Lovisi's *Hardboiled* #22 detailing all the craziness that went on when dealing with the company.

Super-Science Fiction Vol. 1 #1 Dec. 1956 cover by Kelly Freas

man caught in a hail of falling space debris. Pure science fiction. But inside, the contents were far from *Astounding* or *Amazing* in themes. There were no hardcore SF fantasies. You could call the *SSF* story "the working man's science fiction."[2]

In fact, as the magazine approached its final issue in 1958, it had evolved into a SF/horror zine. Its pages thrived on alien monster stories with titles that lacked a bit in the imagination department: "Creatures of Green Slime;" "Beasts of Nightmare Horror;" "Monsters That Once Were Men." This could be why today's SF critics look back at *Super Science Fiction* with such disdain. Milt Subotsky,[3] in his entry for *SSF* in *Science-Fiction, Fantasy, and Weird Fiction Magazines* writes:

"By the end of 1959, there were only nine (existing science fiction magazines). *Super-Science Fiction* . . . was, deservedly so, one of the casualties."

Peter Nichols, in *The Encyclopedia of Science Fiction*[4] (St Martin's Press, 1993), dismisses *SSF* with a curt "its contents were mediocre." This despite the fact that the roster of authors included Robert Silverberg, Harlan Ellison, Robert Bloch, Isaac Asimov, and Jack Vance.

Looking back now, the five stories that made up the first issue of *SSF* were written by virtual unknowns who would later have varying degrees of success. Of course, the two most recognized names, Robert Silverberg and Harlan Ellison, would revolutionize the SF field in the 1960s. Ellison, with his biting wit and thoughtful fiction became the most decorated writer of any genre and continues to this day doling out justice with a pen, aiming at any target that strikes his fancy or raises his ire. Silverberg also became one of the "most imaginative and versatile writers ever to have been involved with SF,"[5] publish-

---

2 In his opening editorial, editor W.W. Scott claims that "the theme of our magazine . . . is people." People who "challenge the skies with . . . cold fury."

3 Yes, *that* Milt Subotsky. The producer responsible for such classy horror pics as *Tales From the Crypt, Vault of Horror,* and *Asylum.* Of course, the guy should also be held responsible for *The Land That Time Forgot* and *At the Earth's Core,* films that make me appreciate *Robot Monster* and *Mesa of Lost Women.*

4 *Science Fiction, Fantasy, and Weird Fiction Magazines,* edited by Marshall B. Tymn and Mike Ashley (Greenwood Press 1985). This is an indispensable volume and should be in any serious genre buff's library. No foolin'.

ing dozens of SF novels during the 1960s and 1970s. Silverberg would contribute three dozen stories during the short life of *SSF*, under his own name and various psuedonyms.

The month after *SSF* #1 went on sale, Henry Slesar would see his first story published in the second issue of *Alfred Hitchcock's Mystery Magazine*. Slesar continued to be a regular throughout the first two decades of *AHMM*, selling hundreds of crime and mystery short stories. He's also well known to digest collectors as the author of the rare and collectible movie tie-in, *20,000,000 Miles to Earth*, published in 1957. Russ Winterbotham went on to write several SF/adventure novels for Monarch, among them *Planet Big Zero*, *The Space Egg*, and *The Red Planet*. Under the name Stephen Marlowe, Milton Lesser created Chester Drum, an FBI agent turned P.I., for a series of novels in the 1960s. The Chester Drum novels became one of the most popular men's adventure series at a time when the book racks were swamped with the likes of The Man From Uncle, Matt Helm, The Destroyer, The Executioner, and, of course, James Bond.

What separates *SSF* from the rest of the pack? An inherent goofiness, bad editing, bad proofreading, and cliches galore. (In fact, the cliches are so apparent that you envision the writer's guidelines read-

Super-Science Fiction Vol. 1 #2 February 1957 cover by Ed Emshwiller

ing something like "Just write like everybody else out there.") Even the pros contributed bad prose. Bloch's "Broomstick Ride" is without doubt one of the worst stories he ever wrote in a sixty-year career. And though he'd become a critic's darling in the 1960s, a lot of Silverberg's stories are comparable to the bad fiction prevalent in science fiction fanzines (sometimes worse).[6] The most imaginative aspect of Silverberg's stories for *SSF* nine out of ten times was the name of the planet his protagonist is visiting.[7] The story is secondary, the characterizations a distant third. Many times Silverberg falls prey to the old SF writer's trick of simply affixing a goofy name to

---

5 Brian Stableford, *The Encyclopedia of Science Fiction* edited by Peter Nicholls. First edition. Doubleday, 1979. Pg. 546.

6 At this time, Silverberg has commented, the author was pumping out 10,000 words a day. In fact, half of the contents of the August 1959 issue were written by Silverberg under his own name and various pseudonyms.

7 Some of the better planet names: Sandoval IX; Vordil IX; Danimar III; World of 1000 Colors; World Seven of Star System A; and my favorite—World 9 of System XG.

something we're all familiar with.

Here's an example, from the subtly-titled "Monsters That Once Were Men" (August 1959):

". . . they looked like things out of a nargheel-smoker's worst nightmares . . . their bodies were unutterably repulsive. I felt like vomiting at the sight of them. Danny Tsung said thickly, 'Of all the sickening sights I ever don't want to see again—'"

With *SSF*, you never knew what you'd run into. Sure, you'd be subjected to prose as "elegant" as:

The Colorful Aliens of SSF

Dozens of aliens invaded the pages of *Super-Science Fiction* over its three year existence. Here are some of the more colorful descriptions:

"They were eight feet tall, thick of body and covered with spines, like some horribly animated cactus . . . Their mouths were the mouths of frogs, flap-lipped and toothless. Their tongues were long, forked, and hinged at the front; their eyes were pocketed atop their oblong skulls."
"Mission: Hypnosis" (Vol. 1 #2)

"It was long—five feet, at least—and otterlike in general form. But there were a half-dozen legs on each side of the brown, furry body and the face vaguely resembled a gorilla's, differing only in the inordinate length of its fangs. The two forward limbs were equipped with huge, formidable pincers."
"Hostile Life-Form" (Vol. 2 #4)

"They looked like giant amphibians, eight or nine feet high as the surf splashed around their flipper-feet . . . at least twenty feet long, standing on six legs . . . half their length seemed to be head. Their mouths were enormous and filled with yellow-green fangs. Their eyes, like twin lamps, gleamed atop their snouts."
"The Loathsome Beasts" (Vol. 3 #6)

"It was about the size of a giraffe, moving on long, wobbly legs and with a tiny head up at the end of a preposterous neck. Only it has six legs and a bunch of writhing tentacles as well, and its eyes, great violet globes, stood out nakedly on the ends of two thick stalks. It must have been twenty feet high."
"Catch 'Em All Alive" (Vol. 1 #1)

"A blur of many-jointed arms . . . with a crushing grip of steel . . . a face of unbelievable horror. A pair of wiry black pincers emerged from a slavering gash in the center of the face, while many-faceted eyes peered inhumanly."
"Horror in Space" (Vol. 3 #2)

"They looked like living corpses, with their white domed skulls and the big staring eyes. One of them had an extra set of limbs sprouting out of the sides of his chest—not arms, but boneless tentacles that flailed around nervously like pale whips. Another had disgusting slimy skin that oozed little blisters of pus."
"Monsters That Once Were Men" (Vol. 3 #5)

"The negative thoughts, inhibitions, both artificial and commonsensed, buzzed around in his head like a swarm of angry gnats—no, more like the fragments of a gyroscopic flywheel that has vibrated apart and lost all its stability; or the neat pattern of iron filings on paper held over a magnet, suddenly deprived of their polarity and scattered by a careless shake."

But then, you'd happen upon passages like this:

"You could always find the biggest crowds around the cage when the keeper dropped a live, kicking slug-beast into the twenty-foot web, and that God-awful hairy body pushed out into the dim light of the cage from its silk-strand-covered hiding place and danced across the thick strands of the web like a ballerina from hell."

Or this:

"Radek sat groggily where he was put, quivering occasionally as the organism within him attempted to regain control over his numbed and useless muscles.

'Sam, can you hear me? Sam?'

'I . . . hear you.'

'Sam, tell me—what's happened to you? What kind of thing has taken you over?'

'I am part of It,' Radek said tonelessly. 'The oneness . . . the fulfillment. All is one here on this world, and I am part of It. Of We.'"

As noted, by the end of its run *SSF* had transformed itself into a BEMzine, chronicling the adventures of astronauts who stray too closely into the giant spider's web on Amalgam-8 or encounter giant fire-breathing centipedes with wings on Boolsheet-4.[8] The April 1959 issue carried the headline: "Special Monster Issue" and spotlighted loathsome beasts and asteroids of horror. All three of the remaining issues carried the "Monster Issue!" banner.

Super-Science Fiction was one of a kind.

Super-Science Fiction Vol. 1 #3 April 1957 cover by Kelly Freas

---

8 I wonder if Stan Lee and Jack Kirby did a lot of *SSF* browsing when it came time to create all those goofy monsters for the Marvel titles of the late 1950s and early 1960s.

Free Trading Cards

For periodic updates about *The Digest Enthusiast* and other Larque Press projects join our email list. Sign up today to receive a set of free *The Digest Enthusiast* Trading Cards while supplies last.

www.larquepress.com

Super-Science Fiction Contents and Synopses

Compiled and summarized by Peter Enfantino

Vol. 1 #1 December 1956
"Catch 'Em All Alive!"
by Robert Silverberg ★★
(5100 wds.) illo: Kelly Freas
Four zoological scientists land on a planet inhabited by strange, exotic beasts. Before long they realize they've set down on an interplanetary zoo and they're the new exhibit representing Earth. Dated now, but still a good read.
"Who Am I?" by Henry Slesar ★★1/2
(10,300 wds) illo: Ed Emshwiller
Two 'space traders' happen upon young Joe Smith drifting in a space sled. When Smith comes to, he explains to the traders that he can't remember how he came to be adrift in space. Turns out that Smith has multiple personalities because of a ritual conducted on an uncharted planet called Othello. The ritual combines the "essence" of several people into one body. Smith has absorbed his ex-shipmates. A rambling, amusing tale that shifts gears every couple of pages or so.
"Psycho at Mid-Point" by Harlan Ellison ★★
(6500 wds) illo: Paul Orban
After a particularly long space voyage, an astronaut apparently loses his mind and goes on a rampage. It's up to one brave crew member to stop the madman before he kills all aboard.
"Chance of a Lifetime"
by Milton Lesser ★★★
(5700 wds) illo: Paul Orban
Mr. and Mrs. Imber decide on a soul transmigration for their latest vacation and have their minds switched with those of a Travarmanian couple. Good solid ending helps this tale of unsubtle prejudice.
"Once Within a Time"
by Russ Winterbotham ★1/2
(9300 wds) illo: Ed Emshwiller
A beautiful woman is sent "back from the future" to prevent a scientist from creating a time machine. Confusing 'time curve' tale.

Vol. 1 #2 February 1957
"Mission: Hypnosis" by Harlan Ellison ★★1/2
(6000 wds) illo: Ed Emshwiller
Laird Barley volunteers for the Goner Squad, an ultra-elite tactical force that cleans up the galaxy. Barley's mission is to deliver a message (hidden deep inside his brain via hypnosis) to the Aldebarenites (aka the Gobbleys for their annoying habit of eating humans). Good twist ending.
"The Great Illusion" by Manly Bannister ★
(5700 wds) illo: Kelly Freas
Cliff Rowley is sent to investigate a world whose civilization may be imaginary. Long and tedious.
"Mr. Loneliness" by Henry Slesar ★★1/2
(1500 wds) illo: Paul Orban
In the future, man has learned new ways to combat loneliness in space.
"Woman's Touch" by Evelyn E. Smith ★★
(6800 wds) illo: Ed Emshwiller
Fairly amusing tale of the first colonists

> "Could an emotion born of propinquity, and desperation approach the meaning of love? The alarm circuits in his brain clanged raucously ... Did this mean that any unusual stress could peel the armor from his naked emotions? If so, he was as vulnerable and unfit to administer as any bearded Venusian sandhog".
>
> "One Woman For Venus" by Winston Marks *SSF* Vol. 1 #3

on a planet of uneducated dwarves and how the newcomers set out to "domesticate" the inhabitants.

"The Untouchable Adolescents" by Ellis Hart ☆☆☆
(5900 wds) illo: Kelly Freas
The crew of the Wallower try to convince the telekinetic inhabitants of a doomed planet that their spaceship is their only hope of survival. Ellis Hart was, in actuality, Harlan Ellison.

"Every Day is Christmas" by James E. Gunn ☆☆☆1/2
(7900 wds) illo: Paul Orban
After three years of solitary confinement, a man comes back to Earth to find that TV advertising has taken over the lives of the populace. Excellent early thesis on the "evils" of television is just as relevant today as it was forty years ago. Gunn had scores of stories published in the SF magazines, including the "Conquest of Space" and "Blood Transfusion" series (which ran, unlike most other series, in various magazines in the mid-fifties). Clute calls "Beyond Bedlam", Gunn's novelette that ran in *Galaxy* in 1961, "brilliant." A James Gunn checklist was published by Chris Drumm in 1984.

"Death of a Mutant" by Charles V. De Vet ☆☆☆☆
(4700 wds) illo: Ed Emshwiller
A young boy has the power of euthanasia with just a touch of his hand. Powerful short story has two qualities not often associated with *SSF* stories: 1) a present-day setting, and 2) a very downbeat ending. The next year, De Vet wrote a monster story, "Special Feature" for *Amazing* (May 1958) that probably would have fit in nicely with the *SSF* "monster issues."

Vol. 1 #3 April 1957

"One Woman For Venus" by Winston Marks ☆
(6000 wds) illo: Kelly Freas
The two occupants of a spaceship en route to Venus, one the new governor, and the other a murderess, find love and happiness among the stars. If Harlequin Romance released a SF novel, it would probably read a lot like this dreadful bore.

"The Rim of Eternity" by Koller Ernst ☆☆
(4200 wds) illo: Paul Orban
Luke Risen, pilot of the experimental X-33 plane, cruises past Mach 40 and finds himself staring at another dimension. Interesting concept falls apart halfway through when Luke holds a silly conversation with his dead wife, who now resides in the 4th dimension. Ernst was just a dabbler in SF fiction (in fact, I can't find any reference to SF writing outside of *SSF*), but he had several crime stories in *Terror Detective*, *Manhunt*, *Double-Action*, *Guilty*, and *Alfred Hitchcock's Mystery Magazine*.

"Pariah Girl" by Boyd Ellanby ☆☆1/2
(3900 wds) illo: Kelly Freas

Super-Science Fiction Vol. 1 #5 August 1957 cover by Kelly Freas

Lt. Charles Bradford hopes to marry an android girl on the planet Hozhan until his application is rejected because the girl is a "criminal." Bradford gets the runaround trying to find out exactly what the girl's crime was, eventually learning during a big Hozhan feast that the girl's a pariah because she won't eat Hozhan's favorite delicacy: Earthmen! Though tame compared to today's bloody tales of cannibalism, "Pariah Girl" is pretty risque stuff for an otherwise fairly clean-cut SF digest. Ellanby was the pseudonym of William C. Boyd and Lyle G. Boyd.

"Brink of Madness" by Arthur Sellings ★★
(6900 wds) illo: Paul Orban
Sam Bishop wakes up from a coma after a car crash that costs him his legs and his memory. Dependent upon his wife Lena, Sam becomes a bitter, paranoid man. What starts off as a promising *Twilight Zone*-type tale degenerates into *Peyton Place* with a silly expository. Sellings later published dozens of shorts (mostly in *New Worlds*) and the acclaimed end-of-the-world novel, *Junk Day* (1970), published posthumously. (Of which John Clute noted it was "peopled with engrossing character types.")

"Galactic Thrill Kids"
by Robert Silverberg ★½
(4000 wds) illo: Ed Emshwiller
Silverberg mixes two genres (science fiction and juvenile delinquency) and ends up with this silly story of a space pilot kidnapped and taken for a joyride by three juvies.

"Invulnerable" by Harlan Ellison ★★★
(7500 wds) illo: Ed Emshwiller
When the government finds out that Eric Limmler is impervious to harm, they convince him to take a dangerous trip to Mars. This affecting story of the lonely life of "the man who can't die" is a good example of the lesser-known material that Harlan Ellison was writing for the SF (and crime) magazines of the 1950s.

"Bright Flowers of Mars"
by Curtis W. Casewit ★★★ (2100 wds)
Worldwide hero David Powers is to be the first man on Mars when his ship is struck by a meteor shower. He fights all odds to patch up the damage and continue his voyage. A science fiction version of "An Occurrence at Owl Creek Bridge," but still an effective read. Casewit had four stories published in *Weird Tales* during the magazine's last three years.

"Hometown"
by Richard Wilson ★★ (800 wds)
Short-short about homesick moon colonists who visit a very realistic Earth facade.

Vol. 1 #4 June 1957

"World of a Thousand Colors"
by Robert Silverberg ★
(5000 wds) illo: Ed Emshwiller
Every millennium (or so) a "test" is held on the World of 1,000 Colors. Jolvar Hollinrede considers the "test" important enough to murder a man in order to take his place at the shindig. This is a story that goes nowhere sloooowly.

"Final Trophy" by Harlan Ellison ★★
(5000 wds) illo: Ed Emshwiller
Big game hunter Nathaniel Derr travels to the planet Ristable to have a showdown with the ultimate beast. Derr plans to add the beast's head to his collection but the natives of Ristable think otherwise. The "shock"

> "He raised his five feet and one hundred and twenty pounds of bone and gristle out of the divan. He smiled with a smirk that made me feel like I needed a shower, and his voice was like oil drained off after ten thousand miles of driving."
>
> "The Abominable Creature" by F. X. Fallon *SSF* Vol. 3 #3

ending is telegraphed in the Emsh drawing that opens the story.

"Desire Woman" by Henry Slesar ★★ (4400 wds) illo: Paul Orban
Clarissa Mahon hires a PI to investigate her space trader husband Mack. Turns out Mack has a girl stashed on another planet—his "desire woman." Clarissa decides enough is enough and heads to Tradepost Four to put a stop to her hubby's philandering ways.

"Pushover Planet" by Don Berry ★★1/2 (9000 wds) illo: Paul Orban
Spacemen investigating the planet Fennel II discover a symbiotic life form that feeds on its host's emotions. Very reminiscent of *The Tingler*, but this bizarre little novelette takes a fork in the road (this way to horror, this way to loonieville) and dispenses some *Marty*-like pathos in its subplot involving the captain and the mousy female science engineer. Despite a letdown climax, still a strange read.

"New Men For Mars"
by Calvin M. Knox ★★★ (12,000 wds) illo: William R. Bowman
Ambitious novelette of a United Nations inspector sent to inspect two colonies living on Mars in huge domes ala *Logan's Run*. Fun, H. G. Wellsian, energetic SF, with a hokey, *Star Trek*-type deux ex machina development in its wrap-up.

"The Well-Fed Birds"
by Richard R. Smith ★★1/2 (3200 wds)
Spacemen are marooned after they crash land on Mars, but find the Martians accommodating hosts. In fact, too accommodating. Nasty climax.

"The Dope" by O. H. Leslie ★★★ (2300 wds)
Amusing tale of a bumbling time traveller who knows nothing about the workings of his time machine. The traveller appears out of the blue (literally) on the doorstep of a gang of impatient doctors who try to gain information from him, only to find that the man is . . . a dope.

Vol. 1 #5 August 1957

"Three Survived" by Robert Silverberg ★★1/2 (11,100 wds) illo: William R. Bowman
Roy Kilbourne thinks he's in big trouble when he escapes his disintegrating spaceship with the only other surviving crew members—two men he considers to be buffoons. When the three land their "escape boat" on an alien planet, it turns out that Kilbourne is the buffoon when it comes to survival. Fun space-opera.

"Alternate Universe" by Robert Bloch ★★1/2 (2700 wds) illo: Paul Orban
Tom Morton creates a drug that induces an alternate universe.

"The Search For Sally"
by A. Bertram Chandler ★ (9500 wds) illo: Ed Emshwiller
A pilot is convinced that his girlfriend, who died in a plane crash, is actually alive and has been kidnapped by Martians. He assumes this because he is convinced she is sending him telepathic messages. Interminably long short story, made worse given the author's reputation in the SF field.

"I'll Take Over" by George Whitley ★1/2 (6300 wds) illo: Paul Orban
A decade before *2001: A Space Odys-*

Super-Science Fiction Vol. 1 #6 October 1957 cover by Kelly Freas

sey, "I'll Take Over" tells the story of a spaceship that learns to think.

"Hunt and Strike" by Raymond E. Banks ☆☆ (5700 wds) illo: Ed Emshwiller
A weapons maker sends the "waspette," a tiny guided missile to the New White House to assassinate the president. Interesting concept trapped in uninteresting prose.

"Twice-Told Tale"
by Theodore L. Thomas ☆[1/2] (2100 wds)
Nathaniel Dove commands a fleet of three rocketships testing the theory of space curvature. Dove is convinced that if he flies straight for 15 years, he'll eventually come back to Earth. He's right, but where did he get a 15-year supply of food and fuel. You gotta wonder about these small details sometimes.

"Invasion Footnote"
by Cordwainer Bird ☆☆ (1600 wds)
An inventor creates the SIMs, small robots he intends to control the world with. Unfortunately for this genius, he makes them too perfect for his own good.

Vol. 1 #6 October 1957

"A Time For Revenge"
by Calvin M. Knox ☆☆[1/2]
(5100 wds) illo: Ed Emshwiller

Mark Fenton heads to Vordil IX to find out why his younger brother was executed. Isaac Asimov, please meet Mike Shayne.

"The Childless Ones"
by Daniel F. Galouye ☆☆
(9500 wds) illo: Ed Emshwiller
On the planet Repugnant-A (yes!), a small group of earthlings try to find the reason why none of the Repugnants (!) have any sexual desire. The resident elderly astronomer discovers that it has something to do with the twenty year cycle of Repugnant-B (an identical rogue planet). About the same time that the men of the expedition get the hots for the sole human female on the planet, the disdainfully obese (and apparently otherwise useless) "Miss Jennifer." An unusually sick and deranged *SSF* tale that repeatedly crosses the line of good taste. In a strangely entertaining way, of course.

"Song of the Axe" by Don Berry ☆
(10,200 wds) illo: Paul Orban
On Procycon IV, the Procys battle the Outsiders for control of their planet and possibly the whole galaxy. With its "full, firm breasts" and plentiful "soft flesh", "Song of the Axe" should have been a contender for "*Spicy Science Fiction Stories Magazine*" (if there had been one), but even the crazed ballet (a religious ritual) and hand-to-hand combat can't save this from being one crashing bore.

"The Fear Trap" by Richard R. Smith ☆
(2500 wds) illo: Paul Orban
Four astronauts break into an ancient Martian tomb and are trapped by a death ray that reduces the men one-by-one to ashes. An incredibly dumb ending.

"Death's Planet" by Robert Silverberg ☆☆
(9600 wds) illo: William R. Bowman
When he's framed for murder, Ree Crawford (or Carpenter; Silverberg can't seem to decide which) flees Velliran disguised as an ecology officer on a flight to explore the deadly "World Seven of Star System A", where anything and everything will kill you. "Death's Planet" comes equipped with a coincidental climax that would stimie even the most gracious of critics. Very reminiscent of Harry Harrison's "Deathworld"

series of novels (the first volume of which was not to see print until 1960).
"The Better Life"
by Charles V. De Vet ★ (2100 wds)
After a miraculous near-death experience, Roy McMahon discovers he can "will" good things to happen. A better job, less cellulite on the wife, good humanitarian things like that. In fact, the only thing McMahon can't get is a satisfactory conclusion to his story since what finishes up "The Better Life" is one of the most abrupt finales ever!

Vol. 2 #1 December 1957

"The Gentle Vultures" by Isaac Asimov ★★ (6000 wds) illo: Ed Emshwiller
Asimov's social commentary about a race of aliens, the Hurrians, who travel from planet to planet, waiting like vultures for civilizations to wipe themselves out. Not an outstanding early example of science fiction from a man who would later see his name in the title of a SF magazine.

"Broomstick Ride" by Robert Bloch ★ (3400 wds) illo: Ed Emshwiller
A scientific expedition on the planet Pyris finds life forms resembling broomstick-riding witches. A rare misfire for Bloch, lacking any of the master's usual suspense or wit.

"The Hunters of Cutwold"
by Calvin M. Knox ★★1/2 (10,800 wds) illo: William R. Bowman
Big game guide Kly Brannon is blackmailed by the heartless Murdoch into leading a tour of ten bloodthirsty quasi-hunters to the pacifistic Nurillons. On the way they encounter the usual deadly beasts, such as the vicious pack of killer blue dogs and the giant man-eating toads. The story's a little too long and a tad too much "man is really *the* animal" preaching for my tastes, but the story still manages to entertain and has a nice wrap-up.

"Get Rich Quick" by Richard R. Smith ★★★ (3400 wds) illo: Paul Orban
Brik's girlfriend travels to Delira, where she discovers a quick and "easy" way to make millions. The Delirans, it seems, are big fight fans and Brik finds out too late that they prefer their fights to the death. Nice, chilling finale leaves ques-

Super-Science Fiction Vol. 2 #1 December 1957 cover by Kelly Freas

tions unanswered, but still satisfies.
"Quarantined Species" by J. F. Bone ★1/2 (5500 wds) illo: Paul Orban
The Horgels are the cutest, furriest little varmints this side of Uranus, but the emotions they stir up in humans can be deadly. Deadly dull, that is.

"Misfit" by Robert Silverberg ★★ (4700 wds) illo: William R. Bowman
Web Foss searches Sandoval IX for his estranged wife, Carol, who's fled Egri V after a heated argument. Now Foss must deal with the Adaptos, a genetically-engineered race designed for the low gravity Sandoval IX, and their reciprocated racist hatred for Earthlings. Yet another preachy tale.

"The Weegil" by Evelyn E. Smith ★★1/2 (4500 wds)
Mrs. Kinnan wins a game show and the prize is a weegil. What's a weegil? Turns out to be an egg-shaped tank (with a scientist inside) sent from Venus to monitor Earthlings. Fair SF with a humorous twist.

Vol. 2 #2 February 1958

"Worlds of Origin" by Jack Vance ★★ (8700 wds) illo: Ed Emshwiller
Magnus Ridolph, Jack Vance's futuristic Hercule Poirot attempts to solve the mysterious murder of Lester Bonfils

Super-Science Fiction Vol. 2 #2 February 1958 cover by Kelly Freas

with help from the ten suspects themselves. "Worlds of Origin" so obviously falls outside of the normal *SSF* story. It's very well written, but the style and humor, along with the whodunit aspects, would fit much better in *Ellery Queen's Mystery Magazine*. The better writing, by the way, does not make it a better story. "Origins" starts out promising but soon becomes very dull. Vance would later become a fan favorite (thanks mostly to his "Dying Earth" saga) and is now one of the most collectible SF authors.

"Secret Weapon" by Arthur Zirul ☆
(9300 wds) illo: Paul Orban
Walter Keegan, agent of BETT (The Bureau of Extra-Terrestrial Trade) sets out for the planet of TTP-1009-4B (hands down, the dumbest of all the dumb planet titles) where the telepathic residents are being held as pawns in the galactic war of the sinister Vegans. Excruciating bore from start to finish.

"The Red, Singing Sands"
by Koller Ernst ☆☆
(4700 wds) illo: Ed Emshwiller
Mars is the setting for this mediocre tale of jealousy and body snatchers.

"Prison Planet" by Robert Silverberg ☆☆¹/²
(11,400 wds) illo: William R. Bowman
The penal planet of Bardins Fall, forgotten by the rest of the galaxy for over 500 years, suddenly seems on the brink of space travel. Nervous about the possibilities of cons in space, the agency known as Space Travel (a galaxy-wide CIA) sends their top assassin, Hale Ridgley, to throw a monkey wrench into Bardins Falls' space exploration program. Though one of Silverberg's best *SSF* stories, "Prison" runs out of gas as it nears its climax.

"The Happy Sleepers"
by Calvin M. Knox ☆☆☆
(3200 wds) illo: William R. Bowman
A Mars rocket somehow touches off a plague of catalepsy on Earth. The sleeping awake in another dimension, a happier one at that. A fun, *Twilight Zone*-type tale which poses the question "which dimension is the real one?"

"The Old Timer" by Richard R. Smith ☆☆
(1700 wds)
Two thugs harass a Martian on a ferry journey.

"Time Travel Inc."
by Robert F. Young ☆☆☆ (1700 wds)
Good short-short about two dolts who travel back in time to settle a biblical wager. Young contributed over 100 stories to the SF digests in the 1950s–1980s.

Vol. 2 #3 April 1958

"Planet of Parasites"
by Calvin M. Knox ☆☆☆
(10,700 wds) illo: William R. Bowman
After over a year-and-a-half of isolation and study on Gamma Crucis VII, you'd think the research team would welcome their replacement team's arrival. But the ten men and women seem to lack all emotion. The new team soon finds out why: the planet itself is actually a parasitic organism that controls the human mind. Reminiscent, obviously, of John Campbell's *Who Goes There?* and Jack Finney's *The Body Snatchers*, "Parasite Planet" still provides an enjoyable read and climaxes in one of the most pessimistic and effective *SSF* fade-outs.

"All the Troubles of the World"
by Isaac Asmov ☆☆
(6200 wds) illo: Ed Emshwiller
In the future, thanks to the massive "Multivac" machine network,

crime has not only been wiped out, it is predicted and prevented while it's still just a thought in the emoter's head. Asimov's mini-version of *1984* has a few neat twists.

"All-Purpose Robot" by Jay Wallace ★
(3900 wds) illo: Paul Orban
Harvey tires of his wife's constant demands so he buys a robot twin to carry out all of his duties. *All* of them. Really bad sitcom SF.

"I Want to Go Home"
by Robert M. Williams ★★★
(3600 wds) illo: Paul Orban
A boy insists to his psychologist that he is actually an alien building a machine to "get myself back home." Then he proves it.

"The Tool of Creation" by J. F. Bone ★★★
(7200 wds) illo: Ed Emshwiller
A crew aboard a spaceship argue theology, unaware that they are about to become a part of creation. Interesting and, yes, thought-provoking tale spends the first half of its length examining various possibilities of creation, almost in a non-fiction form.

"The Seed of Earth"
by Robert Silverberg ★★★½
(4400 wds) illo: William R. Bowman
Barchay rides to the V'Leeg village to seek out the son he sired with an alien maiden twenty years before. Though an obvious morality play (racism rages between Earthman and V'Leeg), "Seed" doesn't get overly preachy and Silverberg remembers that the first order of business in a *SSF* story is to entertain. Easily Silverberg's best story for the magazine.

"The Situation on Sapella Six"
by Harlan Ellison ★ (2900 wds)
Earthman vs. monkey alien on Sapella Six. Ellison may very well be the most decorated and respected writer of this or any other generation, but I doubt if this story will pop up in any of his "Best of" anthologies.

"Pain Reaction" by T. Cogswell & H. Randolph ★★½ (1200 wds)
A short-short shocker about a spy who infiltrates a reaction-speed experiment. The kind of eerie horror story that would have shown up in the pages of *Weird Tales* if that magazine had survived a few more years.

Super-Science Fiction Vol. 2 #3 April 1958 cover by Ed Emshwiller

Vol. 2 #4 June 1958

"Hostile Life-Form"
by Daniel F. Galouye ★★½
(6500 wds) illo: Ed Emshwiller
Captain Parker and his band of intrepid explorers on Vitar-IV discover two life forms: the vicious oterillas (half otter, half gorilla!) and the seemingly domesticated psuedarmadils (which, coincidentally, dine only on oterillas). A real dopey, Disney-type SF first half leads to a fairly gruesome climax after the Earthmen discover the true secret of the psuedarmadils. Nice, nasty final scene.

"Little America on the Moon"
by Arthur J. Burks ★★★
(5800 wds) illo: Ed Emshwiller
Kay Archer has decided to become the first woman to give birth on the moon. Her husband has other ideas. Nicknamed "The Speed Merchant of the Pulps," Burks contributed hundreds of stories to several magazines, both genre and "mainstream." A collection of his horror stories from *Weird Tales* appeared from Arkham House in 1966: *Black Medicine*.

"Slaves of the Tree" by Eric Rodman ★★½
(10,800 wds) illo: William R. Bowman
The five members of the "Examination Squad" head to Maldonad to check out an abandoned colony not

Super-Science Fiction Vol. 2 #4 June 1958 cover by Kelly Freas

heard from in 200 years. What they find is an alien-human crossbreed that worships a gigantic tree. Soon all but one of the squad members fall under the spell of the tree. Hints are dropped that the one squad member who doesn't succumb to the sexual vibes emanating from the idol is either impotent or gay. The big surprise (he's neither) is dropped in a sly twist towards the climax.

"Special Aptitude" by R. H. Hardwick ★★★ (3300 wds) illo: Paul Orban
Aliens invade Earth and use a lottery system to snatch earthlings off to their planet. One man decides to live each day as his last before his number is up. Funny story hands the gigolo his just desserts in the end.

"Frontier Planet" by Calvin M. Knox ★★ (5800 wds) illo: William R. Bowman
The first settlers on Hannebrink IV must

contend with a marauding horde of aliens. With its settlers, "cow-beasts", town meetings, and shoot-outs, "Frontier Planet" is nothing more than a mediocre western dressed up with SF cliches. But even when you put a dress on a pig, it's still a pig.

"No Planet is Safe" by Harlan Ellison ★
(5400 wds) illo: Paul Orban
The men of the Suleiman Agate search in vain for a planet that does not present deadly danger.

"One to a Customer"
by Theodore R. Cogswell ★½
(2200 wds)
Alan Shirey buys a widget from an alien that guarantees he gets his girl and humiliates the guy she's currently involved with.

Vol. 2 #5 August 1958
"A World Called Sunrise"
by Eric Rodman ★★
(11,000 wds) illo: Ed Emshwiller
In the future, victims of radiation poisoning (fairly common, it's pointed out) are rounded up and shipped to another planet light years from Earth. Ryne Rocha, one of the condemned, leads a rebel band to steal a rocket ship and head back to Earth. On the way, the crew stumble on Thagran Dyorm, Commander of the Vengilani Invasion Fleet, ironically on his way to conquer Earth. A fairly exciting space battle leads to a climax that's a direct steal from an old Ray Bradbury short story (the astronaut flaming while re-entering Earth's gravity is viewed below as a shooting star). If I was a high-falutin' literary critic, I'd make deep observations about Silverberg's premonition of a society that treats infected victims like the plague and seeks to isolate them. Since I'm not, I won't.

"The Cold-Blooded Ones"
by Calvin M. Knox ★★
(5400 wds) illo: Ed Emshwiller
Are the lizard-like inhabitants of Xhreena friendly? That's the question a scouting party must answer when it lands on the strangely cold world.

"Many Mansions in the Sky"
by Koller Ernst ★★★
(8400 wds) illo: William R. Bowman

Super-Science Fiction Vol. 2 #5 August 1958 cover by Kelly Freas

Earth has been destroyed by nuclear war and its only surviving children drift through space in the Star Ark, a quasi-Death Star, which houses not only thousands of earthlings, but also farms, buildings, and other earthly amenities. But something's gone wrong with the Ark and it's hurtling back to the burned-out husk of Earth. "Many Mansions" delves into previously uncharted *SSF* territory: religion. Many of the occupants of the Ark feel God is manipulating their every move. Marred only by an embarrassingly corny ending.

"A Planet All My Own"
by Richard F. Watson ★★★
(5100 wds) illo: Paul Orban
George Marks wins an entire planet in the Grand Lottery and decides this would be a good way to get away from it all. Once he gets there though, he discovers the world has one more inhabitant: a telepathic shape-shifter who just wants George to love her. At first he's not reciprocal, but then decides there's nothing to lose. A neat little yarn with a deceptively nasty last line.

"The Gift of Numbers"
by Alan E. Nourse ★★½
(3900 wds) illo: Paul Orban
A bookkeeper is tricked into "trad-

Super-Science Fiction Vol. 1 #6 October 1958 cover by Ed Emshwiller

ing souls" with a con man. Amusing, with a twist ending reminiscent of those that Robert Bloch churned out. Nourse's main claim to fame is that the title of his 1974 novel, *The Bladerunner*, was used by Ridley Scott for the Harrison Ford movie (just the title was used; the story, of course was adapted from Philip K. Dick's *Do Androids Dream of Electric Sheep?*). He also wrote several children's science fiction novels with titles like *Trouble on Titan* (1954) and *Star Surgeon* (1960).

"The Beautiful People" by Austin Hamel ☆ (3700 wds) illo: William R. Bowman
After twenty years in a deep freeze, astronauts Graham and Ian land on the planet of "It" to find dozens of naked people frolicking, bathing, and generally having a good time (leaving out only Volleyball, it seems). The two soon learn that these free spirits are actually "pets" of a higher force. When the higher force finally comes into view, it turns out to be a pair of vicious nimbus clouds (reminding me of one of those 1950s cheapie SF flicks that couldn't afford special effects). This might be Hugh Hefner's idea of SF-fantasy, but I'll take the man-eating plants and giant walruses, thank you. Hamel also wrote crime stories for *Guilty*, *Murder*, and *Manhunt*.

"The Martian Wine"
by Curtis W. Casewit ☆☆ (2200 wds)
Members of the Terra-Mars Trade and Exchange Commission bargain with the monkey-like inhabitants of the Red Planet, attempting to gain access to Martian bubbly. Turns out the joy juice runs through the canals like water. An interesting set-up leads to a surprise climax. The surprise is that there *is* no climax! Literally, "Wine" ends as though the editors either forgot the last manuscript page or they ran out of room in the issue.

Vol. 2 #6 October 1958
"The Fight With the Gorgon"
by Robert Silverberg ☆
(2900 wds) illo: Ed Emshwiller
It's not much of a fight.

"The Painted Ghost" by Richard R. Smith ☆ (4200 wds) illo: Ed Emshwiller
Sam Weeks discovers a race of invisible men on the planet Ceres. Incredibly boring and talky.

"The Untouchables" by Calvin M. Knox ☆$^{1/2}$ (10,600 wds) illo: William R. Bowman
Special Intelligence agent Lloyd Malin is given the assignment of seeking out and exposing the spy hiding out on Dyrain. Another incredibly boring journey to another incredibly boring planet with nary a bit of excitement.

"Nothing's Impossible"
by Charles L. Fontenay ☆
(5700 wds) illo: William R. Bowman
Martha travels to Mars to spend a little time with her Uncle Theodore (who runs a retreat known as The House of Brotherhood). Into Martha's lonely life steps Fors Venturi (known to other Martians as "The Desert Stalker"), a handsome, virile stud whose only peculiarity is that he can walk around Mars without a spacesuit. After the inevitable occurs, Fors tries to convince Martha that she too can cast away her Earthly bonds and breathe "the sweet wine that is Martian air." Will Martha trust this odd, yet handsome, bohunk and toss off her jeans? Will Martha's skin boil and her head explode like Arnie's did in *Total Recall?* Will I ever read a sappier mixture of space and

> "Come on, you hell-thing, you spawn of satan!" he shouted hysterically. "Come and get me, you filthy freak! Catch me if you can, you stinking travesty on nature!"
>
> "The Loathsome Beasts" by Dan Malcolm *SSF* Vol. 3 #6

soap? Fontenay was also the author of the 1964 disaster novel, *The Day the Oceans Overflowed* (Monarch).

"Castaways of Space" by
Dan Malcolm ★★★¹/²
(6300 wds) illo: Paul Orban
Meet Lieutenant McDermott of the Galaxy Patrol Corps. Alcoholic, hates his job as galactic cop, bad attitude. Picture Bruce Willis as McDermott. His latest assignment is to track down Blaine Hassolt, who's kidnapped a senator's daughter and crash-landed his ship on a planet of cat people. The inhabitants worship Hassolt and his captive as their king and queen, and that suits the kidnapper fine. McDermott must figure a way to rescue the girl and get off the planet without being blow-darted by the cat people! Wild pulp fun, "Castaways" is at turns both dopey and sly. It's also got one of the best wrap-ups of any of the *SSF* tales.

"The Great White Gods"
by Wynne N. Whiteford ★★★
(3000 wds) illo: Paul Orban
A mining party made up of Earthmen has been taking advantage of the Ulnis, a primitive race that worships a mythical great white god. For such a short tale, "The Great White Gods" is a very enjoyable read until its abrupt and unsatisfying last paragraph. Author of the apocalyptic novel, *Breathing Space Only* (1980).

"Invasion" by A. Bertram Chandler ★★★
(4800 wds)
The remaining members of an entire civilization cruise the galaxy, looking for an inhabitable planet, ready to conquer if necessary. After years of searching, they come across the perfect planet (guess which one) and begin the invasion that quickly unravels, leaving them at the mercy of . . . (but that would spoil the "surprise that you'll figure out about three-quarters of the way through). Sure, it's predictable, but Chandler (the author of the SF/horror novel *The Sea Beast*) injects enough excitement that it still emerges as a fun little bit.

"Blood By Transit" by Harlan Ellison ★★★
(3000 wds)
Domineering zillionaire Prescott Glowey is dying of a rare blood disease at his home on Mars. He insists that his three business flunkies teleport blood from Earth to gain him a few more years. A very entertaining alternative look at matter teleportation ala *The Fly* (but definitely more gruesome).

Vol. 3 #1 December 1958

"The Aliens Were Haters"
by Robert Silverberg ★★¹/²
(6000 wds) illo: Ed Emshwiller
In the year 2190, America and Brazil have competitive colonies on Kothgir II. A scouting party from each camp happens upon the wreckage of an alien spacecraft and discovers the occupants are the first in a wave of invaders. Gets a bit preachy towards the climax (as a lot of these did) but that doesn't ruin a good read.

"First Man in a Satellite"
by Charles W. Runyon ★★★★
(5600 wds) illo: Ed Emshwiller
Max Canning volunteers to be the first man to orbit Earth in a satellite (more like a sardine can), but regrets it after the vessel is damaged by a meteorite. Nail-biting suspenser reads like a solo *Apollo-13* without the happy ending. *This* is super science fiction. Runyon contributed several stories to *Alfred Hitchcock's Mystery Magazine*, *Manhunt*, and *Mike Shayne Mystery Magazine*.

Super-Science Fiction Vol. 3 #1 December 1958 cover by Kelly Freas

"The Unique and Terrible Compulsion"
by Calvin M. Knox ☆☆
(10,600 wds) illo: William R. Bowman
The Interstellar Merchant Service is fairly sure that Anton Lidman, who runs an outpost on Danneroi, has gone rogue and is supplying drugs to the natives. The IMS sends in Dave Garth to assess the situation. Conrad's *Heart of Darkness* done *SSF*-style, right down to the "the king is dead—long live the king" finale.

"The Fast-Moving Ones" by J. F. Bone ☆
(4000 wds) illo: William R. Bowman
A group of space explorers must deal with a race of super-speed aliens.

"Exiled From Earth"
by Richard F. Watson ☆☆☆¹/²
(4900 wds) illo: Paul Orban
Two hundred years into the future, all forms of entertainment, including theater, are banned on Earth with the passing of the "anti-sin legislation." A traveling theater group roams the galaxy performing Shakespeare for Martians, Venusians, or any alien who will sit still for the Bard. One of the actors yearns to return to Earth, even if it means death. Even though it's set two hundred years into the future and written over fifty years ago, "Exiled" is actually a story ahead of its time, almost as if Silverberg could see the coming of the crazed anti-everything groups of today.

"Creature From Space"
by Harlan Ellison ☆☆☆
(6200 wds) illo: Paul Orban
Another patchwork of *The Thing* and *Invasion of the Body Snatchers*, but this one provides a little originality and a lot of fun. Ellison populates his short tale with an amusing band of "Imbecile Earthlings," the crew of the Ionian Trollop, who must contend with yet another monster loose aboard a ship deep in space. "Creature" reads like a chapter in a bigger work. It would have been interesting to see what Ellison could have cooked up had he written a novel around the Trollop exploits.

"The Utter Stranger"
by Alan E. Nourse ☆ (2400 wds)
An alien begs a science fiction writer to help him convince the US government to fund a "guide beam" to send the alien home. A one-line joke that goes on too long (even for a seven page story), topped off with a ludicrous "infinity" ending.

Vol. 3 #2 February 1959

"Beware the Robot!" by Daniel F. Galouye ☆
(7600 wds) illo: Ed Emshwiller
Euclid the robot stirs up trouble for Drs. Halloran and Richeldorf when it learns the secret of time travel. A total snoozer, with nothing to recommend but some snatches of loony dialog.

"Horror in Space" by James Rosenquest ☆☆
(7200 wds) illo: Ed Emshwiller
An old-fashioned "monster on the loose in the spaceship" story. A giant shape-shifting cockroach is terrorizing the crew of a spaceship in deep space. A low-budget *Alien*, with doses of *Who Goes There?* and *Them* thrown in for good measure.

"A Place Beyond the Stars"
by Tom Godwin ☆☆
(7600 wds) illo: William R. Bowman
A "dark star" will destroy the world in 2550. Five hundred years before, scientists send out search parties to locate habitable worlds as way-stations to an inevitable Earth-II. Fair SF yarn with a neat intro: a chapter from a book detailing the Earth's destruction and aftermath. Godwin's most famous story, according to John Clute, is the grim

Super-Science Fiction Vol. 3 #2 February 1959 cover by Ed Emshwiller

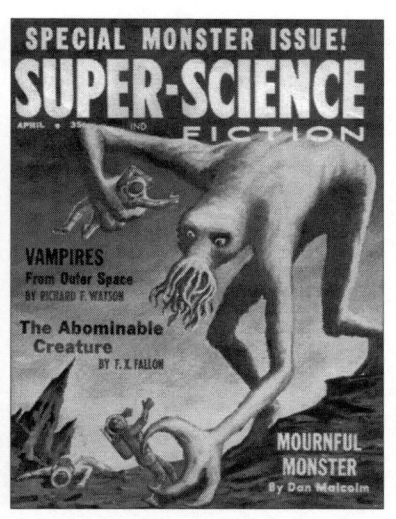

Super-Science Fiction Vol. 3 #3 April 1959 cover by Ed Emshwiller

SF tale, "The Cold Equations" (*Amazing* August 1954), wherein a female stowaway is jettisoned from a spaceship.
"Waters of Forgetfulness"
by Eric Rodman ☆☆
(11,800 wds) illo: William R. Bowman
The luxury space-liner James P. Drew (a galactic Titanic) is crippled in space and only a handful of survivors escape to a nearby planet. On the planet, they drink from a stream that corrodes their brains and leaves them in a zombie-like stupor (I felt somewhat the same way after reading all these stories!). Enter Lt. Halderson of the Disaster Patrol to the rescue. Only problem is: by this time they don't want to be rescued.
"Re-Conditioned Human"
by Robert Silverberg ☆1/2
(4900 wds) illo: Paul Orban
Intergalactic jewel thief Nat Hamlin is "re-conditioned" into good guy Paul Macy. His re-hab completely erases bad impulses, but his bad guy past comes a'calling in the form of Dan Helgerson, one of Nat/Paul's old henchmen. Helgerson attempts to blackmail Nat/Paul into rejoining the gang while the reader attempts to stay awake.
"Ego-Transfer Machine"
by George H. Smith ☆ (1400 wds)
A dimwit is tricked into a mind-swapping experiment. Smith, who wrote under his own name and a vast number of pseudonyms, would later go on to write a couple of well known (to paperback collectors at least) novels, *Doomsday Wing* (Monarch 1963) and the cult favorite *The Coming of the Rats* (Pike 1961), as well as a good number of soft porn paperbacks.

Vol. 3 #3 April 1959
"Mournful Monster" by Dan Malcolm ☆☆1/2
(11,400 wds) illo: Ed Emshwiller
On the planet Loki, a tropical and mostly uncharted planet, a small group of plane crash survivors must make their way through a jungle teeming with vicious monsters. Though sketchily written, the story still delivers on the big monster thrills.
"The Abominable Creature"
by F. X. Fallon ☆☆☆
(7000 wds) illo: Ed Emshwiller
That old SF chestnut, the intergalactic zookeeper, is dusted off for good measure. Clem Linton brings zookeeper Big Mike Sill to see the most incredible space animal in the universe: an amoeba that can mime its intended victim.
"Vampires From Outer Space"
by Richard F. Watson ☆1/2
(11,200 wds) illo: Ed Emshwiller
"Brother should love brother despite the fact that he has wings, six-inch

Super-Science Fiction Vol. 3 #4 June 1959 cover by Kelly Freas

fangs, and might drink your blood" is the moral of this dreary story. In the future, Earth has been re-dubbed Terran and has become the stomping grounds for all sorts of alien races, including The Nirotans, hideous grotesqueries in the form of giant bats. The main character is a futuristic Columbo who finds the real killer and spends the last few pages in expository.

"The Huge and Hideous Beasts"
by James Rosenquest ☆1/2
(6900 wds) illo: Ed Emshwiller
Explorers on the planet Giganta find . . . what else? Gigantic monsters! Rosenquest's story actually seems like two tales. The first, a fairly exciting narrative of the spacemen vs. the big bugaboo. The second is a tedious science lecture. The Emsh illo is delightfully gruesome, but as usual, gives away much of the "surprise." Not that there could be many surprises in a story titled "The Huge and Hideous Beasts!"

"A Cry for Help" by Eric Rodman ☆1/2
(5300 wds) illo: Ed Emshwiller
An exploratory expedition to World 9 of System XG finds nothing out of the ordinary until they receive a cry for help from the forest. When they answer the plea, it turns out there is a superior race living on the planet that wants nothing to do with humans.

Vol. 3 #4 June 1959

"Terror of the Undead Corpses"
by Russell Thompson ☆☆☆
(6400 wds) illo: Ed Emshwiller
The first manned expedition to Venus comes under attack by an alien that takes over its host's body and fills it with a disgusting jelly-like substance. A thinly-veiled rip-off of *Who Goes There?* is nonetheless a fairly exciting gothic horror space opera with some very grisly scenes.

"Creatures of Green Slime"
by James Rosenquest ☆☆☆
(6800 wds) illo: Ed Emshwiller
One of the members of a Mars expedition is infected with a growth that gradually envelops his body. Turns out the growth is a life-form feeding off the man, preparing for multiplication. Gruesome, with a delightfully sickening final scene.

"The Day the Monsters Broke Loose" by Robert Silverberg ☆☆☆
(5700 wds) illo: Ed Emshwiller
Silverberg's homage to big monster flicks (which were winding down at about this time) also throws in the obligatory "man is savage" references to our despicable love for violent sport. Jim Barstow travels to far-off planets to capture savage beasts and sells them to promoters who use them in "Monster vs. Monster" arena shows. Though preachy at times, the story still contains a good deal of excitement culminating in a *King Kong*-like climax. Incidentally, the title is false advertising since only *one* monster actually breaks loose.

"Beasts of Nightmare Horror"
by Richard F. Watson ☆☆1/2
(11,000 wds) illo: Ed Emshwiller
Trouble's a'brewin' for the Cameron colony on Danimor III when a big batch of illusionary monsters stalk the streets, destroying all in their path. It's up to the Interstellar Patrol (a United Nations Peacekeeping Squad of the future) to save the day.

"Mating Instinct"
by Lloyd Biggle, Jr. ☆☆ (4600 wds)
Goofy blending of SF and true confessions has a homely woman answering a mental call from her "dream-man", in reality a six-armed alien out to conquer Earth. Biggle also

wrote the SF/horror tale "The Botticelli Horror" (*Fantastic* March 1960).

"The Enormous Diamond"
by Bill Wesley ★¹/² (6000 wds)
Clyde Sanders and his lovely wife Connie, on a honeymoon space cruise, visit the marketplace world of Ceres (aka the Casbah), where they run across a strange shopkeeper and his wondrous diamond. The gem has the power to grow to enormous proportions and does so on their trip back to Earth, endangering all aboard. "Diamond" starts out interesting enough, but then takes an incredibly hokey side trip in its climax. It's the odd story out in that there is no giant monster even though this issue is billed as the "Second Monster Issue."

Vol. 3 #5 August 1959
"The Horror in the Attic"
by Alex Merriman ★★¹/²
(4800 wds) illo: Ed Emshwiller
A young couple, eloping in the middle of the night, seek shelter from a torrential downpour in an abandoned farmhouse, not realizing that it is home to an ancient evil. Dopey and nothing new, but fun nonetheless. Odd story for *SSF* in that there is no futuristic or otherworldy setting. Just a horrific menace.

"Monsters That Once Were Men"
by Eric Rodman ★
(5800 wds) illo: Ed Emshwiller
The obligatory space party lands on an uncharted planet and happens upon the wreckage of the legendary lost ship "Empress of the Sun," which disappeared under mysterious circumstances thirty years before. Inhabiting the ship are the descendants of the survivors of the Empress, mutated by the planet's ghastly radiation into malformed cannibals. Starts out hum-drum and goes nowhere slowly. Full of some wonderfully bad writing and questionable science.

"Birth of a Monster" by Richard Stark ★¹/²
(2100 wds) illo: Ed Emshwiller
Doctor Lamming is summoned to a strange estate to witness the birth of a vampire. Like "The Horror in the Attic," this is an out-and-out horror story, and not a very good one at that. Stark (a pseudonym of highly respected crime

Super-Science Fiction Vol. 3 #5 August 1959 cover by Ed Emshwiller

novelist Donald E. Westlake) would later go on to become the author of the acclaimed Parker series of novels.

"Man-Hunting Robot"
by James Rosenquest ★★
(5800 wds) illo: Ed Emshwiller
Otherworldly version of "The Most Dangerous Game" is fairly entertaining.

"Planet of the Angry Giants"
by Dirk Clinton ★★¹/²
(10,600 wds) illo: Ed Emshwiller
The peace between earthlings and eleven foot aliens on Dunhill V is jeopardized when two selfish interplanetary big-game hunters kidnap four of the giants and take them back to Earth. Good adventure tale ends on a downbeat note.

"World of Creeping Terror" by J. W. Rose ★¹/²
(5100 wds) illo: Ed Emshwiller
The planet Flora is supposed to be inhabited by friendly creatures, but the title tells you otherwise, doesn't it?

"Which Was the Monster?"
by Dan Malcolm ★★★
(5100 wds) illo: Ed Emshwiller
Far into the future, Earth is at war with the Vengilan Confederation while the pacifistic Gysls look on. Ben Chase, an intergalactic spy is en route to earth from Zenuon with an important message encoded in his brain (shades of *Johnny Mnemonic*), when he is forced

Super-Science Fiction Vol. 3 #6 October 1959 cover by Ed Emshwiller

to land on a small planet by a Gysl ship commandeered by the evil Vengilans. An interesting tale that has a thoughtful climax in which Chase must make a disturbing but necessary decision.

"Specimens" by George H. Smith ☆☆
(900 wds)
Amusing short-short about a rocket returning to Earth from Venus.

Vol. 3 #6 October 1959

"The Loathsome Beasts"
by Dan Malcolm ☆☆¹/²
(10,900 wds) illo: Ed Emshwiller
Mark Foster, head of the Springfield Defense Council (located on the Terran-colony world of Lincoln) is called back home from an important luncheon after hundreds of loathsome beasts rise from the ocean and consume mass quantities of nekkid bathers (though the Emsh illo plainly shows them clad in bathing suits). Two of the fatalities include Mark's wife and daughter, so the deluge becomes personal. Unfortunately, Mark can't get help from Earth and the colonists must face the sea monsters with their wits and a few flame throwers. A gruesome, sometimes sadistic space monster tale. Maybe that's why I liked it. The bloody opening siege proves conclusively what scholars have up to now only hinted at: that Peter Benchley grew up reading *SSF*.

"The Monsters Came By Night"
by Charles D. Hammer ☆☆¹/²
(3400 wds) illo: Ed Emshwiller
Emil Gustafson savagely murders a Martian for his diamond jewelry. When Emil gets back to Earth, he's haunted by the Martian's ghost.

"Asteroid of Horror"
by James Rosenquest ☆☆
(6200 wds) illo: Ed Emshwiller
Spaceships are disappearing without a trace, so Mike O'Shea is dispatched into space to find out what gives. Mike crash lands on an asteroid close to the sun, whereupon lives a grotesquerie hard to imagine or describe. Well, okay, it's a big centipede-thingie with teeth. Some interesting bits (a possible tie to Earthly abductions and a particularly harrowing childhood memory) can't liven up what is essentially the same old *SSF* story. Throw in an ending so sappy I believe it was later used on *Eight Is Enough*, and you get snoozeville. An interesting note: Emsh's illo for the story is based on the Kelly Freas cover painting for the June 1959 issue of *SSF*.

"Flying Saucers in the Sea" by F. X. Fallon ☆
(6300 wds) illo: Ed Emshwiller
Treasure seekers Ted Sutton and Paul Mason happen upon a flying saucer on an underwater ledge. Ted becomes obsessed with the craft and soon finds himself equipped with gills. The laughable exchange between Paul and fish-dude Ted toward the climax of the story brings to mind *The Incredible Mr. Limpet*.

"The Great Secret"
by George H. Smith ☆☆ (900 wds)
A description of this story would probably be longer than the story itself (and probably more interesting). Blackmail + seeing the future = hohum.

"The Insidious Invaders"
by Eric Rodman ☆¹/²
(5100 wds) illo: Ed Emshwiller
What begins as an uncanny political prediction: "After the incident of the disposal unit, there was no room for reasonable doubt: something peculiar had happened to Ted Kennedy," becomes just another boring rip-off

of *Invasion of the Body Snatchers*. Ted Kennedy returns from five years on Altair-VI to visit his kid sister Marge, who immediately recognizes there is something wrong with big bro. Quicker than you can say Chappaquiddick, Ted's dropping his jeans (and his genes) to assimilate his sis and her husband. "Ted Kennedy never knew what hit him." Wow, do you think Jeanne Dixon wrote fiction under the Eric Rodman psuedonym?
"The Man Who Could Levitate"
by Abraham Stern ★
(8400 wds) illo: Paul Orban
Can a levitating window washer find happiness in our cruel world? Evidentally, he can. What a poor note to go out on.

Note: Story word counts, rounded to nearest hundred, are culled from *The Index of Science Fiction Magazines 1951–1965* (J. Ben Stark, Publisher, 1968), compiled by Norm Metcalf.

AUTHOR INDEX

Note: Robert Silverberg appeared in every issue under his own name and/or the psuedonyms Dirk Clinton, Calvin M. Knox, Winston Marks, Alex Merriman, Eric Rodman, and Richard F. Watson.

Asimov, Isaac 2/1; 2/3
Banister, Manly 1/2
Banks, Raymond E. 1/5
Berry, Don 1/4; 1/6
Biggle, Lloyd Jr. 3/4
Bloch, Robert 1/5; 2/1
Bone, J. F. 2/1; 2/3; 3/1
Burks, Arthur J. 2/4
Casewit, Curtis W. 1/3; 2/5
Chandler, A. Bertram .1/5
(as by George Whitley) 2/6
Cogswell, Theodore R. 2/3; 2/4
De Vet, Charles V. 1/2; 1/6
Ellanby, Boyd 1/3
Ellison, Harlan (aka Ellis Hart and Cordwainer Bird) 1/1; 1/2; 1/3; 1/4; 1/5;
 . . . . 2/3; 2/4; 2/6; 3/1
Ernst, Koller 1/3; 2/2; 2/5
Fallon, F. X. 3/3; 3/6
Fontenay, Charles L. 2/6
Galouye, Daniel F. 1/6; 2/4; 3/2
Godwin, Tom 3/2
Gunn, James E. 1/2
Hamel, Austin 2/5
Hammer, Charles D. 3/6
Hardwick, R. H. 2/4
Lesser, Milton 1/1
Nourse, Alan E. 2/5; 3/1
Randolph H(al) 2/3
Rose, J. W. 3/5
Rosenquest, James 3/2; 3/3; 3/4; 3/5; 3/6
Runyon, Charles W. 3/1
Sellings, Arthur 1/3
Slesar, Henry 1/1; 1/2; 1/3; 1/4
(as by O. H. Leslie) 1/4
Smith, Evelyn E. 1/2; 2/1
Smith, George H. 3/2; 3/5; 3/6
Smith, Richard R. 1/4; 1/6; 2/1; 2/2; 2/6
Stark, Richard 3/5
Stern, Abraham 3/6
Thomas, Theodore L. .1/5
Thompson, Russell 3/4
Vance, Jack 2/2
Wallace, Jay 2/3
Wesley, Bill 3/4
Whiteford, Wynne N. .2/6
Williams, Robert M. 2/3
Wilson, Richard 1/3
Winterbotham 1/1
Young Robert F. 2/2
Zirul, Arthur 2/2

Follow The Digest Enthusiast on Pinterest for current releases and classic digest magazine covers in full color.
pinterest.com/richardkrauss/the-digest-enthusiast

Like The Digest Enthusiast page on Facebook to add updates on the world of digest magazines to your FB feed.
facebook.com/thedigestenthusiast/

Popular Fiction Periodicals by Jeff Canja
Review by Richard Krauss

Bookseller Jeff Canja is well known to collectors of paperback books and periodicals. His monthly Modern Age Books catalogs are so much fun to peruse, they're practically collectables themselves. His visual approach, a zine/catalog hybrid, with page-after-page of cover repros, is always a pleasure to find in your mailbox.

With years of experience immersed in collectables it's no surprise Canja is also the author of two pivotal reference books on his areas of expertise, one for paperbacks and another for magazines. His *Popular Fiction Periodicals: A Collectors' Guide to Vintage Pulps, Digests, and Magazines* debuted in 2005 and a second edition was published in 2009. The book was a finalist in the History: Media/Entertainment category of the International Book Awards in 2012.

After a one-page introduction, Canja defines the volume's purpose succinctly in "About This Book:" ". . . an essential reference for magazine and book collectors . . . and anyone else with an interest in the popular fiction or magazine artwork of the twentieth century." I'd say it succeeds remarkably well.

"A Brief History of American Popular Fiction Periodicals" provides an excellent overview that correlates the rise and evolution of mainstream fiction magazines in the context of their sourcing, production, distribution and marketplace dependencies. From the earliest entry in England in 1704 (Daniel Defoe's *Weekly Review*), through the Story Papers of the 1800s, Dime Novels and paperback "libraries" of the mid- to late-1800s, the twentieth century's pulp magazines, followed by comic books and paperbacks, the popular digest format of the 1950s and early 1960s, the men's adventure boom, the rise of the true detective (true crime) category, the "true strange" era (*Fate, Search,* etc.), men's entertainment (*Playboy, Gent,* et al) and finally today's few remaining stalwarts of newsstand fiction (Dell's titles and *F&SF*); Canja traces the history of popular periodicals. His essay is loaded with fascinating facts and figures. "At that time [1731] magazine was commonly understood to mean a storehouse for good or supplies. Accordingly, *Gentleman's* [*Magazine*] defined itself as a repository or storehouse for the best writing of the day."

"True detective magazines were not as widely read as the men's adventure magazines, but in the 1940s and early 1950s when they were most popular, the leading titles consistently reported circulations of 200,000 to more than 500,000 copies."

"By the mid-1960s, the digests and other publications that had survived or succeeded pulp magazines in the popular fiction arena were well in decline, and unlike all previous eras, no new type of fiction periodical emerged to take their place." Of course, print and digital books continue to flourish, but Canja's observation pertains to periodicals with a substantial portion of their content devoted to fiction.

The marketplace defines the value of collectables. Canja rightly defines the marketplace for popular periodicals as "thin." Even a highly prized title may change hands infrequently, making it difficult to assign an accurate value. The body of the book is not a price guide. It's a price reference, its values listed from actual sales of each item included. And because the data comes from the author's own transactions through Modern Age Books, there's a consistency in the condition listed that would not be present if the data were collected from a larger pool such as sales from ebay.

That's also why unlike a price guide, not every book is listed. "If a particular issue of a magazine is not included in the price listings, you will often be able to find other issues or other magazines that are essentially comparable for pricing purposes."

Although there are many similarities between the different types of magazines, values are also affected by their differences. For example the age and production values of a pulp magazine make it inherently more difficult to find a "newsstand fresh" copy than say, a digest magazine. Factors like condition, genre, cover art and artist, authors, publishers and titles and even the position in the run can affect value. Canja breaks out each category of magazine: pulps, digests, men's adventure, true detective, men's entertainment and humor and highlights which factors most influence their values.

Cover art and artists are an important part of collecting—for some the *most* important part. The "Cover Art Gallery" presents three covers each for 125 popular cover

192 | Keyhole Detective **POPULAR FICTION PERIODICALS**

Keyhole Mystery Magazine - 4/60    Keyhole Mystery Magazine - 6/60    Keyhole Detective - 9/62

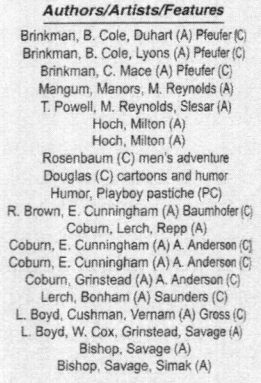

Title - Date	Vol.	No.	Type	Cond.	Price	Authors/Artists/Features
Keyhole Detective - 6/62	2	3	Dgst	VGF	$33.00 A	Brinkman, B. Cole, Duhart (A) Pfeufer (C)
Keyhole Detective - 6/62	2	3	Dgst	VGF+	$20.00 A	Brinkman, B. Cole, Lyons (A) Pfeufer (C)
Keyhole Detective - 9/62	2	4	Dgst (P)	AF	$27.00 A	Brinkman, C. Mace (A) Pfeufer (C)
Killers Mystery Story - 11/56		2	Dgst	VG-	$17.00	Mangum, Manors, M. Reynolds (A)
Killers Mystery Story - 1/57		3	Dgst (P)	VG	$26.00 A	T. Powell, M. Reynolds, Slesar (A)
Killers Mystery Story - 3/57		4	Dgst (P)	VG+	$47.00 A	Hoch, Milton (A)
Killers Mystery Story - 3/57		4	Dgst (P)	G	$7.00	Hoch, Milton (A)
King - 3/71	1	1	Mag	VGF	$10.00	Rosenbaum (C) men's adventure
Laff Time - 11/64	7	7	Dgst (P)	VG+	$5.00	Douglas (C) cartoons and humor
Laffboy - 2/65	1	1	Mag (P)	VG	$11.00 A	Humor, Playboy pastiche (PC)
Lariat - 11/38	11	5	Pulp (A)	VG+	$19.00 A	R. Brown, E. Cunningham (A) Baumhofer (C)
Lariat - 9/41	12	9	Pulp	VGF	$25.00	Coburn, Lerch, Repp (A)
Lariat - 1/42	12	11	Pulp	VGF	$33.00 A	Coburn, E. Cunningham (A) A. Anderson (C)
Lariat - 7/42	13	2	Pulp	VGF+	$29.00 A	Coburn, E. Cunningham (A) A. Anderson (C)
Lariat - 3/43	13	6	Pulp	VGF	$40.00 A	Coburn, Grinstead (A) A. Anderson (C)
Lariat - 1/45	14	5	Pulp (A)	VGF	$40.00 A	Lerch, Bonham (A) Saunders (C)
Lariat - 3/45	14	6	Pulp (A)	VG+	$27.00 A	L. Boyd, Cushman, Vernam (A) Gross (C)
Lariat - 5/45	14	7	Pulp (P)	VGF	$44.00 A	L. Boyd, W. Cox, Grinstead, Savage (A)
Lariat - 7/45	14	8	Pulp (P)	VG+	$40.00 A	Bishop, Savage (A)
Lariat - 3/46	14	12	Pulp	VG+	$24.00 A	Bishop, Savage, Simak (A)

Killers Mystery Story - 1/57    Killers Mystery Story - 3/57    Laff Time - 11/64

artists, over 43 pages, encompassing images from 1910 to 1973.

To preface the Price List section, Canja details the meaning of each aspect of a listing. This includes title and date, volume and number, condition, price, and author, artist and feature information. Of course, condition is a major factor and two pages are devoted to defining it. "The grading terminology in this book is often used by dealers and collectors...." In fact, an article on ebay, "Grading the

Condition of Vintage Paperbacks & Pulps" includes Canja's definitions as one of two outstanding references; the other being *Hancer's Price Guide to Paperback Books*.

It's unfortunate there isn't a single standard for condition, but until an overarching authority emerges collectors' must either develop relationships with booksellers whom they trust will accurately grade their wares, see the items in person, or study photographs online carefully to determine condition on their own terms. As Canja recommends "When buying by mail or online, you should feel free to ask the seller for condition details."

Canja's grading system provides seven categories appropriate to his subject: Fine, About Fine, Very Good to Fine, Very Good Plus, Very Good, Good and Good Minus, with Very Good occupying the widest range of acceptable general wear and minor flaws.

The Price Listing runs just under 200 pages and includes six cover images and twenty item entries on every page. I find the reference invaluable and consult it frequently as I add to my digest library and research titles for articles. It's rare to run across a title that is not represented.

The prices listed represent a snapshot in time—today a seven-year-old snapshot. Scarce items and those in top condition have increased in value, but those in average grades, not so much; unless there's something that adds to their demand such as a popular cover artist. Canja advises readers to use the list as one source of information to arrive at a fair price. In many cases I find the prices are still relevant, and certainly useful in relative terms comparing one item to another.

The volume also includes two eight-page sections of full color covers, bringing the total cover image count to over 1,800.

The final features include a two-page list of "Author Pseudonyms;" five pages of "Other Resources" listing magazines, books, other price guides and shows; a list of all the titles included, along with their genre and format; an alphabetical list of cover images with their page number; and a four-page bibliography. Indexes include one for Authors and one for Illustrators.

Popular Fiction Periodicals is 6" x 9," perfect bound, 362 pages. The book is no longer in print, but a few copies are still available directly from the publisher. Send $29.95 to:
Glenmoor Publishing
PO Box 325
East Lansing, MI 48826
(Mention *The Digest Enthusiast* with your order to receive free shipping.)

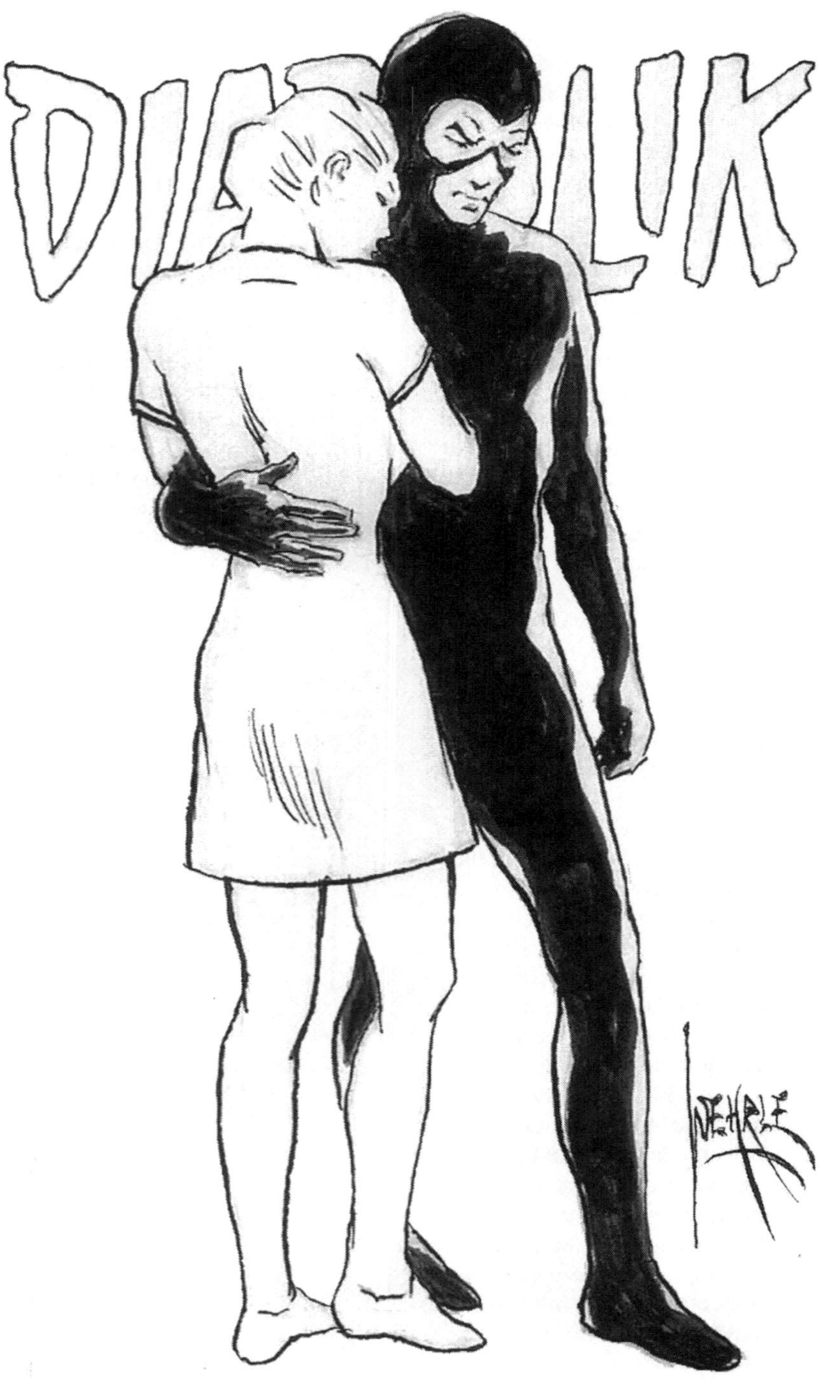

Diabolik-al Digests
Article and portraits by Joe Wehrle, Jr.

"Diabolik is not a clear-cut figure, but just the opposite. He battles against concepts and facts in a fashion that reminds us of a primitive justice."
Tony Raiola, *Diabolik* No. 1, November 1986 Pacific Comics Club

Diabolik! Dark, sinister apparition of the night! Relentless in quest for fortune; clever and cautious in technique. Always a step ahead of those whom he has set his sights on. Is he friend or foe? He might prove to be either. Or both.

This bizarre, black-clad figure first made his appearance at Italian newsstands in November, 1962, the creation, oddly enough, of two Italian sisters, Angela and Luciana Giussani.

Angela (1922–1987) is actually the initial intellect behind Diabolik. In her younger years she worked as a model, but became involved in publishing when she married Gino Sansoni, contributing to a series of magazines he was publishing at the time.

Later she created her own company, Astorina, and published the first Diabolik episode. Angela herself is credited with writing fifty-five issues of *Diabolik*. Her sister Luciana (1928–2001) began collaborating on stories with issue number thirteen, and continued to write many episodes solo after Angela's death in 1987. She carried on directing the fortunes of Diabolik until 1999, two years before her own death.

Diabolik is a master thief, ruthless in his pursuits, but he primarily preys on criminals. He is rather profoundly a genius, with broad knowledge of science and mechanics, using his mastery of chemistry to create incredibly lifelike disguises. He constantly

Angela Giussani.

changes his identity by employing a wide array of fleshlike masks which conform perfectly to his face, and he uses similar masks to alter the identity of others as well.

Orphaned as a child, Diabolik grew to manhood on an obscure island used as a criminal base, where he studied his future trade under the tutelage of the rough inhabitants there. He later was responsible for the death of the leader of the outlaw group.

For weapons, Diabolik often uses daggers, which he wields with exceptional skill, and sometimes employs a small dart gun with projectiles which leave the victim unconscious.

Diabolik met his future partner in crime and lover, Eva Kant, in the third issue. Worthy companion to our anti-hero, she scrupulously follows Diabolik's direction, and never shies from theft or killing. Eva's steely glances dart from narrowed eyes, beneath a crown of golden hair pulled into an extreme bun at the back of her head. Diabolik's eyes are usually narrowed as well, and together they give one an impression of a couple diabolically preordained for each other.

A third character ever-present in the saga is one Inspector Ginko. Ginko, in his own way as taciturn as Diabolik himself, is obsessed with bringing the criminal to justice, even though Diabolik's activities often serve to bring many of Ginko's other investigations to a close, without, of course, the troublesome necessity of a trial.

Understand, I am really not very fluent in the Italian language, but I have accumulated quite a number of Italian comics through the years, beginning in the 1960s, when there were no decent reprint books available in this country of the old classic newspaper strips. The Italians were reprinting a wealth of material from the 1930s and 1940s, and I learned, if imperfectly, to figure out the story lines and much of the dialogue in their comics.

Luciana Giussani.

One of the most interesting (and most complicated) Diabolik stories centers around a young woman, Adele, responsible for the keeping of a valuable cache of gems. Aldo, her fiancé, aided by Monica, his new mistress, plots to betray Adele and enrich himself. Diabolik, who also has an interest in the gems, holds Adele safely and comfortably in a secluded location, while Eva impersonates her for a switch of the valuables. Later, Aldo, walking along the street with several other people, is surprised to see Monica apparently drive up, exit her car and approach him. But it isn't Monica, it is Eva in a mask. She shoots Aldo point-blank and drives off. The real Monica is, of course,

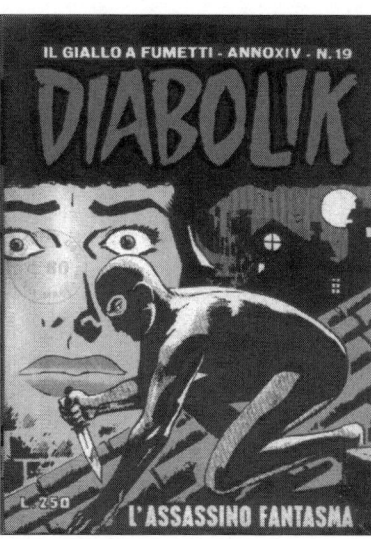

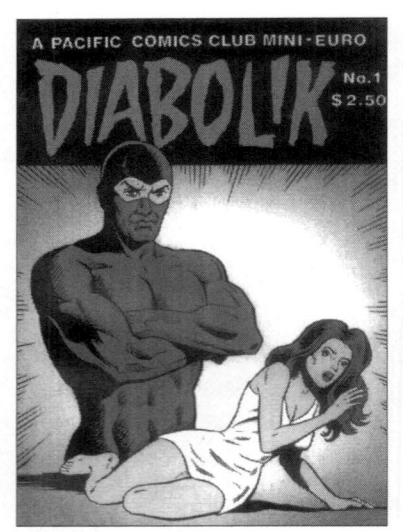

Diabolik #1 November 1986

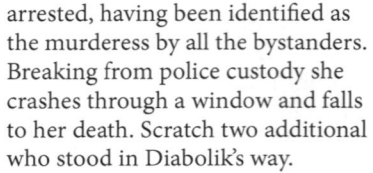

Diabolik #2 November 1986

arrested, having been identified as the murderess by all the bystanders. Breaking from police custody she crashes through a window and falls to her death. Scratch two additional who stood in Diabolik's way.

I doubt a story line of this sort would pass the Comics Code if published in America, but I've learned of no effort to assign any blame to Diabolik for corrupting the youth of the countries where the comic is distributed.

In 1986, Tony Raiola's Pacific Comics Club released two Diabolik digests with English translations. Pacific Comics Club was already noted for its reprints of American newspaper strips like Flash Gordon, Buck Rogers and Dick Tracy. Tony was probably hoping that the *Diabolik* reprints would be as successful, but since there have been no additional releases, the series must not have found an audience here, and that's too bad, because the two issued are typically quick-paced and absorbing. An interesting arc in the second has Diabolik (in disguise) wearing glasses in which mini versions of his dart gun have been installed in both temples. Posing as a hotel clerk, he gains entrance to two mob members' room, stuns one with the device, and when the second one asks, "What happened?" he answers, "Your friend seems to be ill." As the guy approaches to check things out, Diabolik touches the other temple of his glasses frame, and the man promptly crumples. I can think of times when I would like to have had a pair of these glasses.

A film, *Danger: Diabolik* was released in 1968 in Italy. There have also been, at various times, a cartoon series, a radio show, and a video game. And more than a hundred and fifty million copies of the digest comic have been sold!

The Rail City Rolls
Science fiction by Ron Fortier

A mobile city racing through the Rocky Mountains is suddenly under attack by hostile forces armed with sophistocated weaponry.

The alarm klaxon sounded throughout the ten levels of Car Seven, waking young Alet Eams from a sound sleep. He lifted his head off the pillow just as Fireman Second Class, Dario Rasco shoved the barracks door open and started screaming.

"To stations, you wet-eared rookies, we're under attack!"

In the nanosecond it took for that last word to register, Alet was throwing off his covers and tumbling out of his bunk, along with the ten other cadets in his unit. He scrambled to throw on his gray jump suit with the red piping and fastened the black tool belt about his middle. He slipped into his work boots, the Velcro seals kissing the second he tapped them, then he was scrambling out the door behind Cadets Erlo Murr and Demi Washu. Somehow no matter how many drills he went through, they always bested him in reaching the outside corridor.

But now the yellow emergency arrows were pointing up, not down, and for the time the green cadets realized this wasn't a drill but the real thing. The Capitol Class Spirit of St. Louis was actually under attack by hostile forces and they were being pressed into its defenses.

Frantically Alet climbed up the emergency ladders taking them up to the twelfth and final level to the roof. He could see two Fire Chiefs, their chevrons embroidered on their black jump suits, waiting on the staging ramp, the closed steel iris over their heads.

"Move out you green beans," the one with the brown beard snarled as Erlo hoisted himself to the small, half moon platform. "Grab your ear-plugs and mango-slippers and get out there!"

Following Demi, Alet grabbed a set of com-plugs and stuffed them into his ears at the same time he reached out and took a set of mango-grips from the second Chief, this one missing an eye, a livid red scar running over a milky white orb. *Sheet . . . that's Chief One-Eye Sharn!!!* The man was a living legend among the twenty-thousand citizens of the great train.

"Whatcha looking at, boy?" Sharn growled, slapping the rubber coated shoe magnets into his hands.

"Nothing, Fire Chief!"

"Then put on your shoes and move out!"

Suddenly a bracing gust of cold air washed over him and Alet gulped, losing his breath for a second. The roof iris had circled open and the wind, whipping over the giant cars at two hundred and thirty miles an hour tore at him like a living demon. Thankfully all recruits, men and women, wore their hair cut to the scalp.

He grabbed the ladder, somehow having edged between Erlo and Demi and was the second to pop out of the hatch onto the rushing hell that was the roof of the racing city train. And just like that his senses were assailed from the buffeting wind that threatened to rip him off the curved steel roof to the sights of the majestic Rocky Mountains the train was moving through like a fast moving bullet. Ahead of him was a plasti-bubble gun turret with two mounted .80 caliber canons. There was room for two gunners in each of the six blisters atop each separate car.

"*Attention defense forces,*" the voice cut into his ears from the tiny comm-plugs. "*Two dozen single engine airhawks are attempting to raid our supplies. These are mountain based pirates. FIRE AT WILL!*"

Airhawks!! Alet had never seen a flying machine in his sixteen years of life. That was all about to change.

"LOOK OUT!"

He jerked his head up against the hitting wind in time to see a body coming at him, its arms and legs akimbo. Erlo, already half in the gun blister, pulled his arm, yanking him to his knees as the hurtling, screaming, dying cadet went shooting past, off the train and into oblivion beyond.

Falling into the blister, Alet looked up at Erlo, who was six months older, and clearly much wiser. "Jerk greenie didn't fasten his mango-shoes."

And just like that the poor fool had been torn off the train to his death out there . . . somewhere, off the train.

"*Here they come, heading southwest. Orientation, nine o'clock!*"

Alet dropped in the hard bucket seat, snapped on his safety belt while Erlo, his back to him did the same. The older cadet then slapped the Rotational On switch. Now the two of them would be able to spin to right or left in a complete 180 degrees as needed.

By the luck of the draw, Erlo was facing the high mountains and it was Alet looking to the south in time to spot the black dots skimming over the verdant valley below. As they moved over trees, boulders, clear running streams, their shapes crystallized into mosquito like machines with four stationary wings, two to either side of the cockpit where a pilot was lying prone, hands clasped on gun controls. Onwards they flew, climbing higher with each passing yard, until Alet could see their steel-beak snouts were machine gun noses.

The first two airhawks swooped over them, their guns plastering a tattoo of bing along the car's side and then smacking into the plasti-blister. Alet screamed, one hand coming up in front of his face as the tiny spider-cracks rippled over the blister and the airhawk's underbelly whooshed by him.

"Start shooting, you idiot!" Erlo yelled, pressing his own firing studs, igniting his guns to spit out two hundred rounds of hot lead after the retreating aircraft. The second was attacking now and this time Alet opened his eyes and fired.

The mechanical bird was overhead and clear. He'd missed. Erlo kicked his rudder, sending their blister in a spin in time to see three more airhawks come skimming over the train's topside, following its trajectory.

"Alert," Erlo warned into his com-mic, "they're going after shadowing us!"

Alet had a clear shot, he pulled on his gun grip and squeezed as the chain of warbirds swooped overhead. He watched in stunned disbelief as his bullets trailed upward and hit the fragile looking flier until one hit the fuel tank and the tiny one man craft exploded. One second it was a thing of lethal beauty and the next it was a fireball of millions of pieces of blazing hot shrapnel that rained down on them.

The remaining airhawks peeled off.

"Yahoo, we got one!" Erlo called out. "Alet shot it out of the air!"

"*Way to go, cadet. Ev-eryone stay sharp.*"

Just then another airhawk dropped out of the heavens and fired at them. Alet looked up into the face of a girl no older than him, her visage tight in a grim mask as she glared at him from her cockpit.

The blister cracked and a huge chunk broke away, a tiny sliver hitting Alet's cheek, drawing blood. "Aagh."

"Alet, you all right?" Erlo feeling the air, calling over his shoulder, voice tinged with fear.

"Yeah," he finally replied. "But that was too close for comfort."

And just like that the air was free and clear, with white cotton mountains the only umbrella over their world. The Spirit of St. Louis cleared the Rockies and ahead was a vast, open plain reaching to the horizon.

"*Attention, all clear! This is an all clear. Return to duty stations.*"

Alet signed, his hands trembling. He reached up to touch the smear of blood on his cheek, holding up his painted fingertips. Beyond he could just make out the mighty fusion engine that pulled his world.

There was another ping in his ear-jack. "*Oh, and Happy Birthday Cadet Eams. And well done.*"

The body rested on the side of a rocky slop facing the east. The life force within it was ripped free when it was hurled off the train at a speed in excess of two hundred and thirty miles an hour. The lungs couldn't fill with air and when it hit that unforgiving ground, the back and neck snapped, the boy's consciousness ending upon impact. So it was a lifeless husk that rolled over, very much a broken thing of muscles, blood and bones until it came to a stop, its torso up, the unseeing eyes looking east. The useless ears unaware of the train's rumblings as it vanished through the mountain passes, leaving him to the elements.

Nature arrived with the sand ants who, by their curious ways, quickly covered the dead thing, moving in and out of the gray jumpsuit, exploring every inch of the rapidly cooling flesh. Slowly they began to feast.

They were followed by the various bugs that also came to eat and prosper from the bounty provided for them by the whims of fate. Then as the sun began fall behind the mountain peaks to the west, the timid and ever hungry wolves appeared.

All the while the open, unseeing eyes recording nothing of this beautiful chain of life. After all, it was just a corpse.

It has once been Cadet Macri Tern.

Cardinal Conductor Inge Kenaux looked up at the stars through the plexi-dome atop the viewing platform and marveled at their beauty. Even at maximum speed, there was no better place aboard the mighty Spirit of St. Louis, that provided him with such peace and serenity. It was at night when the blasted world was lost to sight, that he would come here and sit alone, deep in prayer and reflection. Here amidst the splash of the shining constellations, he would find strength to endure his mission as the spiritual leader of his flock, The Passengers.

A quick glance at his write chronometer revealed the lateness of the hour and he still had much to do before he could retire.

The attack by the sky pirates earlier was still buzzing through the multiple neighbor cars, his flock both nervous and anxious. They had lost one of the young firemen cadets and it was his job to comfort them, to somehow make sense out of the senseless. Deep within his chest a sigh was born as for the millionth time he wondered what had ever possessed him to join the Conductor Class? He could have gone on to Engineering College like his brother, Manine, and dealt with simple physical issues, with machinery and grease guns, with fusion generators and mango-navigation. Anything but the complexities of the human heart.

Slowly he rose out of the plush viewing chair and made his way to the elevator. At fifty-six, he'd started developing a pot-belly which was starting to become a hindrance in his mobility. But then again, what was one to do when one's mate was the Managing Director of a Hydroponic Car? Jarcy Kenaux didn't only know how to grow magnificent gardens, she was an excellent chef in her own right. The Cardinal Conductor smiled as he dropped three levels to the floor on which their cozy apartment was located and gave some thought to starting a new exercise routine in the coming weeks. Good health was fundamental to his projecting a spiritual surety others could emulate. After all, sloth and gluttony were sins.

Entering his apartment, he found it dark and empty save for the glow-globe suspended over the kitchen area. Jarcy had left a note on the table that his dinner was in the magno-cooker and that she would be home late. He recalled she'd mentioned something about new cross-root transplants she and her staff were developing to grow bigger mineral rich veggies.

He removed his jacket and clerical collar, before throwing the plastic wrapped plate into the cooker. Three minutes later, seated alone at the small round table, he enjoyed his dinner. When finished, he cleaned up and went into his private office.

The floating glow-globe over his desk brightened as he sat back in his padded chair. He activated his personal computer and punched in the next day's schedule. At the top of the list, after Morning PA Prayers were the words, Memorial Service, Engine Central. Inge Kenaux removed his bifocals and rubbed his tired, brown eyes.

Well, here we go.

"Computer, give me the file sheet on Fireman Cadet Macri Tern."

The screen blinked, the schedule dissolved to be replaced by lines of biographical data and a 3D image of a handsome young man. Kenaux tapped a digital display and the image became a hologram revolving over his desk.

The Cardinal Conductor put on his glasses, leaned closer to the screen and began learning all he could about the young man who had died that morning defending his family, his friends and the Great Train, Spirit of St. Louis. Had he been a true hero or rather some innocent lad trying to find his place on the rails of life? That he died in a clumsy and tragic accident was doubly painful for the man whose job it was to protect the passengers.

The report indicated young Tern had exited onto the roof of the giant train without his magno-boots and been instantly swept away, his life snuffed out in mere seconds. His world of dreams, his loving parents' treasure of immortality, now gone, ripped off the racing train like so much flotsam, caught in the whirlwind of existence.

So much for heroism.

He heard a noise from beyond the door and rightly assumed Jarcy was home. She entered his office after a gentle knock.

"I wish you wouldn't do that," he muttered as she entered the light of the glow-globe, still attired in her green jump suit with white piping. Her gray hair was tight in a bun at the back of her neck and there were still dirt smudges on her beautiful cheeks.

"Do what, your Holiness," she joked, coming around the desk to stand behind him, her hand reaching out for his.

"Knock. Or call me that. I am anything but holy."

She leaned over and kissed his thinning hair atop his head. "You are the holiest man I know, Inge Kaneau. Stop being so stubborn and accept your fate. Or is it faith?"

He held her hand and squeezed. "I do so love you. You know that."

"As sure as water and sun will raise a seed to flower." She saw the still turning hologram. "Is that him, the boy who died?"

"Yes, Macri Tern. I was about to start writing his eulogy."

"Then I'll leave you to it."

"You know I hate this."

"Only because you love, my darling. Death is always riding the rails, isn't that what the Conductor's Good Book says."

She gave him another kiss on the head and then started to leave.

"Thank you."

At the door, "You're welcome. Did you eat your dinner?"

"Yes, it was delicious . . . as always."

"Good. Write your words of pain and loss and then come to bed."

The door slid shut behind her, he still smelling her body and the earth scents captured in her artificial gardens, much like an artificial womb.

The Cardinal Conductor began to transcribe his lament.

Thousands of miles away, beneath the rising moon, the gray wolves, filled with young Macri Tern, bayed their own mournful song.

↙ ↓

A professional writer for over thirty-five years, **Ron Fortier** has worked on comic book projects such as The Hulk, Popeye, Rambo and Peter Pan; with The Green Hornet and The Terminator (with Alex Ross) being his two most popular series. He penned two TSR fantasy novels with Ardath Mayhar, and in 2001 had his first play, a World War II romantic comedy, produced.

Ron currently writes and produces pulp novels and short stories for a wide range of publishers; and has several movie scripts floating around Hollywood looking for a home. If that isn't enough, he also writes Pulp Fiction Reviews, online at: pulpfictionreviews.blogspot.com

A devoted grandfather of six, at 68, Ron is thrilled to be part of the new web-comic evolution. Part of this joy is in the realization of a life long dream, that of becoming a pulp writer. For news about Ron's many projects visit airship27.com

"Due to variations of scale, the "Floating Clarke Monolith" is a bit less impressive on some planets than others."

Betty Fedora #2
Review by Richard Krauss

As a fan of crime fiction digests, my first double-take at this edition of *Betty Fedora* connected in a heart throb. Smack title: She's new, but her wink to her hardboiled/noir roots is unmistakeable. Killer attitude: "Kickass Women in Crime Fiction!" Works for writers and characters and readers—no problem here, sister. Standup cover: Eyes or bust? It took me a sec to catch the lady's dirty little hands, but there's no questioning her invitation to look under the covers.

This may not be your first Betty. Editor Kristen Valentine makes that perfectly clear in her short introduction that welcomes back several contributors, and welcomes anew several more. Somewhat surprisingly they're not all women. But the leads are, and that gives readers something else to think about—how men and women write their female leads and their male support cast.

Shane Simmons starts the dance with "Heads Will Roll." Two women have settled into their lives in the vicinity of a truck stop. One's the waitress at Kelly's Diner, and the other's a bit simple, scrounging turnpike trash for whatever it's worth to pay her way. Problem comes when Earl shows up. Strong characters and crisp dialogue. Drifters come and go, but the real story is the one about the people who stay. In addition to his shorts, Simmons writes scripts for screens and comic books.

"Last Chance Saloon" reflects the English spellings and localization of Brit wit Tess Makeovesky. It concerns a womanizer, Jeff—quite wicked about it, making his Marys until he bores, then moving onto greener maidens. Very successful till he crosses the centerline with the narrator, who shares her aversion of his exploits. Makeovesky stories are proliferating, and a novel, *Raise the Blade*, is due in 2016 from Caffeine Nights.

Colleen Quinn's "Lucifer" features richly drawn characters with caustic roots that define who they became. The adventure takes PI Kit Greene to an isolated farmhouse in Iowa to bust a blackmail scheme.

KICKASS WOMEN IN CRIME FICTION!

BETTY FEDORA

ISSUE TWO

The setup is excellent but for me the climatic confrontation was a bit too congenial. Strong writing with imaginative descriptions and details keep it in the plus column.

A New York native, Quinn's stories appear in numerous anthologies.

Thomas Pluck transports us to a swanky Caribbean resort in "Mannish Water," where racketeers and scammers sometimes land amongst vacationers. A barmaid with dreams meets a dude she calls the Moon Man and they try to help each other out of their respective situations. The setting is as interesting as the characters in this island drama—and that's a good thing. Pluck is the author of *Blade of Dishonor* and numerous other fictional works.

That other ocean's popular island chain is the site of the next crime scene. An Hawaiian attorney's defense of a Hilo drug dealer threatens to sink her career in "Luxury to Die For" by Albert Tucher. It's a terrific balance of plot and story, with enough action to speed the read, enough depth to enliven the cast, and enough tropical cites to put us right there on the breach. The issue's highlight. Tucher is the creator of the series character, Diana Andrews, a prostitute who appears in forty stories, with three novels forthcoming.

The mother/daughter dynamic mixes it up with a police detective/private eye conflict in the context of a serial murder case in "A Diet Rich in Noir" by Lara Alonso Corona. This one emphasizes the characters and their relationships, but still delivers enough forward motion to solve the murders. Corona's growing roster of work appears online and in print.

As its title might lead you to believe, "Burden of Proof" by John H. Dromey, takes place in a courtroom. A purse snatching case in which the accused is so confident of his vindication that it actually goes to trial. The truth is revealed through the exacting dialogue between the witness, the prosecutor and the judge. Dromey is a veteran of *Alfred Hitchcock's Mystery Magazine*, *Plan B* and many other fiction venues.

A contract killer uncovers more than her assignment for her client in "All Things Violent" by Nikki Dolson. Conflicting agendas are further complicated by the killer's mentor and a burgeoning romance. This one takes some nice unexpected twists before the final trigger pull. Dolson's work can also be found in *Thuglit*, *Northville Review* and *Red Rock Review*.

In "Sensible Sleaze" by Sarah M. Chen, an "Ugly Betty" and her hot, blonde sister split for the evening over the after-party for the *Zombies Unloaded* premiere—the low-rent wonder that gave their former cafe coworker a dubious start in movie production, on his way to a real film career. Unfortunately, the bouncers won't let the pitiful girl in, so she waits outside poking at her phone in a lame attempt to orchestrate her plan to cement her relationship with movie boy, and ensure competition from her hot sister is far removed. As you might expect, things get complicated and somebody ends up deadly. Chen has stories in many of today's short run/POD crime anthology magazines and has a novella, *Cleaning Up Finn*, due from All Due Respect Books in May 2016.

At 5" x 8" *Betty Fedora* makes one beautiful package. Her classic 144-page figure pays tribute to the best of her forerunners. But she's cast her own style—and sister, it's one you won't soon forget. I look forward to seeing her again, real soon.

Betty Fedora is available in print and digital formats from amazon.com
For more Betty visit bettyfedora.com

Bestseller Mystery

Hammett Homicides
by Dashiell Hammett

"Who doesn't read him misses much of modern America." DOROTHY PARKER

25¢

Bestseller Mystery B81 December 20, 1946

"I found Paddy the Mex in Jean Larrouy's dive. Paddy—an amiable con man who looked like the King of Spain—showed me his big white teeth in a smile, pushed a chair out for me with one foot, and told the girl who shared his table:"

The Big Knock-Over by Dashiell Hammett

Hammett Homicides: The Dashiell Hammett Digests
Article by Steve Carper

The paperback revolution started in 1937. Two years before Robert de Graff launched Pocket Books with James Hilton's *Lost Horizon*, the noir classic from James M. Cain, *The Postman Always Rings Twice*, appeared as American Mercury Book #1. *The American Mercury* was, at least in memory, a potent name. H. L. Mencken and George Jean Nation launched *The American Mercury* magazine in 1924 with the aim of making it the "gaudiest and damnedest" review of American politics and culture. They succeeded for a decade, but the Depression hit the money-losing magazine hard. Mencken resigned as editor in 1933 and the next year it was sold off by its publisher, Alfred A. Knopf, to Pete Palmer. With Lawrence E. Spivak as his business manager, Palmer cut the magazine to digest size, hoping to ape the success of the phenomenon that was *Reader's Digest*.

Palmer and Spivak looked to less high-brow and therefore presumably better-selling publications to supplement and fund their main attraction just as Mencken and Nathan had. They bought the pulp called *Black Mask* in 1920 to prop up their earlier, snootier money-losing magazine *The Smart Set*. (Low-brow was where the money was: they sold *Black Mask* eight months later for twenty times what they paid.) Pulps were still the backbone of fiction magazines during the Depression years, but Spivak looked to the digest presses the magazine was printed on and saw an inexpensive way to leverage their down time for his existing distribution network. He launched Mercury Publications in 1937 and soon took over the whole Mercury empire.

The American Mercury Book (Mercury Book after #3) was a rapid success. Though the early names reads like a roll of Nobel Prize winners, including Sinclair Lewis, Rudyard Kipling, Pearl S. Buck, and John Steinbeck, the line offered mostly adventure and romance in the classic sense. Another noir classic, Don Tracy's *Criss-Cross*, was #9, but their turning point came in April 1940 with #27, Ellery Queen's *The Dutch Shoe Mystery*. Queen, the joint pseudonym used by Frederick Dannay and Manfred B. Lee, was among the handful of bestselling mystery authors in America and would become a perennial million seller in paperback. More Queens were followed by the other members of the bestsellers club, Agatha Christie, Erle Stanley Gardner, and Rex Stout, and with #35 the line became, forthrightly, Mercury Mystery. Spivak created a companion line called Bestseller Library at the beginning of 1940 and #1 and #3 were both books of Queen short stories. With #17, the name changed to Bestseller Mystery. Spivak's third line was a total surrender: Mercury Detective Books appeared in 1942 with Queen's *The Chinese Orange Mystery*. This obvious descriptor lasted no time, though. With #2 it became Jonathan Press Book and from #3 onward Jonathan Press Mystery. All three mystery lines were essentially interchangeable: the same authors, sometimes with the same titles, could be found scattered through each. Ads at the back of the books listed titles from all three under the general heading of Mercury Mysteries. The three were similar in their size, their colored flimsy heavy paper covers, and their general emphasis of text rather than illustrations for covers, although line drawings by art director George Salter appeared on Mercury and Jonathan Press. Buyers probably looked at them like a connected and continuous line of magazines to be picked up automatically every month. Spivak reinforced this in the fall of 1941 with a mystery magazine of remarkably similar appearance except that it was saddle-stitched rather than perfect bound: *Ellery Queen's Mystery Magazine* (EQMM).

The Dannay half of Queen was dotty about mystery short stories. He would spend a very large chunk of his royalties amassing the most nearly complete collection of hardbacks containing mystery short stories (in the largest, most all-encompassing sense of mystery) that ever will be assembled and reprinted dozens of lost classics in the magazine. The collection can be found today at the Harry Ransom Humanities Research Center at the University of Texas, Austin. Since 1941 was the centennial of Edgar Allan Poe's seminal "The Murder in the Rue Morgue," rightly or wrongly acclaimed as the first mystery short story, he dug into his trove to produce the largest and deepest anthology of the history of mystery short stories to that day, *101 Years' Entertainment* (yes, 101—that's inclusive) and planned a new anthology annually.

The Queens were not pulpsters,

though a few of their short stories originated in some pulps in the 1930s. *101 Years' Entertainment* doesn't contain a single pulp story, in fact, out of 50 otherwise spanning the field. They insisted that the mystery was merely a literary product that concerned in some fashion a crime, and would offer proof of this as the 1950 anthology *The Literature of Crime: Stories by World-Famous Authors*. They badly wanted a non-pulp magazine that those world-famous authors would not be embarrassed to be seen in. In 1933 (at a time, admittedly, when their own prose style was still too primitive to be rightly included—although they did anyway) they started *Mystery League*, "on a shoestring" as Lee later said. They had literally no staff other than themselves and no budget to attract mere big-name mystery writers let alone *litterateurs*. It lasted four issues, making it a scarce collectible today.

Everything about the mystery world and their personal fortunes changed over the next eight years. Their incomes included sales of their books to Hollywood, serializations in mainstream magazines like *Redbook* and *Cosmopolitan*, paperbacks from a multitude of publishers, *Ellery Queen* comic books, and a high-rated radio show. Mysteries were the hottest trend in the book business in 1941. They had the backing of a real publisher. The economy was roaring back. The "experiment," as the editorial in the first issue termed it, succeeded as well as splitting the atom. *EQMM* quickly turned to gold in those glory years. It immediately became—and stayed—the premiere magazine in the field. The magazine published new work from every cel-

Bestseller Mystery B40 June 15, 1943

ebrated name in the field, reprinted even more celebrated names from outside the field, and made a policy of running a "first story" from a new author in every issue, creating a horde of future celebrated names. *EQMM* was Dannay's baby from the start. Lee handled the writing for the pair, using detailed outlines Dannay created, and had little interest in editing the work of others or any of the other thousand chores that editing involves. From here on, I'll use Dannay whenever I mean the editing half of Ellery Queen and Queen for the brand name of the duo.

Having a star writer, productive editor, and acknowledged expert in the history of the genre as an employee and colleague boosted Spivak's position in the field. Dannay became increasingly important to his business and consequently influential in his decision making. So if Dannay had a mania about short story collections Spivak was happy to oblige him, even though collections of mystery short stories had a dismal reputation in publishing. Only a handful of hardback publishers issued them and only a smaller handlet of paperbacks reprinted short story collections. Printing original paperback collections with no hardback edition to drive sales was unimaginable. Yet Dannay so wanted his favorite authors' shorts to be available that he eventually created a series called Ellery Queen Selects that included Stuart Palmer's *The Riddles of Hildegarde Withers*, John Dickson Carr's *Dr. Fell, Detective, and Other Stories*, Roy Vickers' *The Department of Dead Ends*, Rex Stout's *Not Quite Dead Enough*, and Margery Allingham's *The Case Book of Mr. Campion*. For decades most of these collections were completists' dreams and nightmares. Not only were they the true first editions but they were the literal only editions, not reprinted in any format, a tribute surely to how poorly they sold and how small their audience. My copy of the Carr, snatched up at a wallet-busting $17 in the dim past, was the only one I ever saw before the Internet era.

Only one name in the genre might be an exception. Everybody who read mysteries wanted more. Heck, everybody in America who read wanted more. Nothing more was forthcoming, hadn't been since a surprisingly abrupt end in 1934. Yet dozens of short pieces, a half million words, lay moldering in long-forgotten pulps and lesser magazines, the majority never reprinted in any form. This trove was the lost gold mine of publishing. For Dannay and for Spivak, each for his own reasons and temptations, Dashiell Hammett was the ultimate prize.

Samuel Dashiell Hammett was born in southern Maryland on May 27, 1894. The unusual middle name was that of his mother's mother. She pronounced it da-SHEEL, but the kid was nicknamed Dash from an early age and that syllable triumphed. The family moved around but settled in Baltimore. Hammett's schooling ended with a semester in high school, the Baltimore Polytechnic Institute, whose most famous alumnus was H. L. Mencken. Coincidence, but watch as all the names in my introduction echo through Hammett's life.

The Pinkerton National Detective Agency's Baltimore office, located fatefully in the Continental Building, hired Hammett in 1915 for a salary of $21 a week. He worked under James Wright, "short, squat, tough-talking," in Hammett biographer Richard Layman's description. Interruptions for World War I and a bad case of tuberculosis reduced his actual active duty for the Pinkertons to maybe three years out of the next six, but his experiences and the exotic yet earthy personalities he encountered would color his writing, a new variation on what it meant to be American, and in the long run far more influential than the Jazz Age neurotics of Fitzgerald or the stoic depressives of Hemingway.

In 1922, otherwise unable to work, and with a wife and a year-old daughter in a small San Francisco apartment, Hammett started writing. He aimed high. His first pieces, some fiction, some non-fiction, appeared in *The Smart Set*. Those were not his forte, and he soon found a proper home in *Black Mask* with a long succession of stories about a short, squat, tough-talking nameless operative for the

Continental Detective Agency.

Hammett's name would be forgotten today except by cultists if he stuck to the pulps. Even he disdained them and much of the company he kept. He wanted respectability, he wanted recognition and acclaim, he wanted out of the game and its low pay and the attendant hurried mediocrity that churning out pulp as a living required. He sent his first novel-length piece about his detective, serialized in *Black Mask*, to the prestigious publishing firm Alfred A. Knopf. Blanche Knopf, Alfred's wife, was his champion and first editor. She got him to depulp some of the over-the-top action and cut the number of murders to twenty-four. *Red Harvest* sold well and received the reviews that any and every writer could only wish for. *The Dain Curse* sold better, *The Maltese Falcon* was a much-reprinted and never to be topped revolution, which gave momentum to *The Glass Key* and *The Thin Man*, not as great but still wonderful. And then nothing. After 1934 Hammett's public suffered almost as much as his publisher by his lack of new material, Knopf's agony all-the-greater for the advances that garnered nothing in return except increasingly thin promises and excuses.

Hammett lived the life that his dreams were made of, drinking astounding amounts of now-legal liquor, throwing week-long parties, leaving his wife for a series of mistresses and shorter stays, acquiring his first case of gonorrhea, and staying in penthouse suites of the best hotels, all paid for by the incomprehensible sums of money that Hollywood threw at him. He is a legend of rock-and-roll excess decades early,

Bestseller Mystery B50 April 14, 1944

and the toll was identical. He soon stopped writing anything that wasn't frivolous—a few screen stories and the dialog for the comic strip *Secret Agent X-9*—and then nothing at all.

The rapacious industry that made money off Hammett disguised his failures for years. Hollywood made movies from his novels, radio adapted them into plays. William Powell made furious objections to being typecast as yet another detective when chosen to play Nick Charles in *The Thin Man*, yet MGM's touch made the B-movie into an A-list blockbuster with five sequels and, starting July 1941, a radio show called *The Adventures of the Thin Man* that lasted ten years. John Huston performed the same magic with the third movie version of *The Maltese Falcon*, released in October 1941. A second movie version of *The Glass Key* hit screens in 1942. With Hammett hotter than ever, Knopf put out *The Complete Dashiell Hammett* in 1942 and Pocket Books made

Bestseller Mystery B62 April 13, 1945

them available by the millions when reprinting them, starting in 1943.

That was it. Nothing was left to be picked on his bones and no new work could be expected: the Army had incomprehensibly accepted the 48-year-old underweight, tubercular, suspected Communist when he voluntarily enlisted on September 17, 1942. Nothing, except the short stories that Hammett had for years pretended not to exist, a relic of his early years, not quite fit for the man acclaimed to be the equal of Hemingway.

Dannay well understood the power of Hammett's name. He got Hammett to write a new story, one of his last half-dozen, for the first issue of *Mystery League* and reprinted Hammett stories in *101 Years' Entertainment* and the first issue of EQMM. He would reprint dozens of other Hammett tales in *EQMM* and his many anthologies over the next two decades. Hammett knew his worth as well. In 1947 he responded to a Dannay story request with a terse letter saying only "I agree to accept a fee equal to the highest fee paid to any other contributor to this anthology." Dannay wanted to hold in his hands a book of Hammett short stories. Spivak wanted Hammett in any form possible.

The record is silent but separately or together, they concocted a plan that would ease Hammett's shorts back into print. Their first book of short stories wouldn't be a book of short stories. It would be a Hammett novel.

They may have gotten the idea from talking to people at Knopf. Back in 1929, when Hammett hadn't yet started raking in Hollywood money, he wanted to justify an advance against royalties, so he wrote to Harry Block, a Knopf editor he frequently worked with, suggesting some quickie books of short stories. *Red Harvest* and *The Dain Curse* had been a series of connected stories and he pointed out that "The Big Knockover" and "$106,000 Blood Money" would work in the same way. Alternatively, he touted a collection of short stories to be titled *The Continental Op*. He may have looked seriously into the latter. Hammett's papers are in the Harry Ransom Humanities Research Center alongside Dannay's book collection. They show *Black Mask* paste-ups from five Op stories, "Bodies Piled Up," "The Gatewood Caper," "The Golden Horseshoe," "Night Shots," and "Women, Politics and Murder," under the title *Including Murder*. He quickly withdrew the offer, though, because he felt that he needed to rewrite the stories to make them suitable for book publication and he was deep in better projects, though none of the ones he mentioned were ever finished.

That's likely to be a major clue to Hammett's willingness to accept the arrangement in 1943. Digest novels reputation was a skosh higher than pulps but still far from the rarefied air of Alfred A. Knopf, Publisher. Expectations would certainly be lower and polishing the crudeness out of early works unnecessary. In any case, he gave his assent and on June 15, 1943, Bestseller Mystery B40, *$106,000 Blood Money*, successor to B39, Agatha Christie's *The Boomerang Clue*, and predecessor to B41, Georges Simenon's *The Flemish Shop*, appeared on newsstands.

Care was taken to disguise the fact that two separate short stories had been combined. No mention of "The Big Knockover" appeared anywhere in the volume, even though it is the first and longer half. One copyright date covered both. The second story, the original "$106,000 Blood Money," is merely labeled "Part II" and given separate chapter numbers. (Oddly, the designation "Part I" was left off the front.) When Vincent Starrett wrote an article on the worth of mysteries for the October 1943 *Rotarian* magazine, he said, "Greatly to the delight of admirers of Dashiell Hammett, the toughest and most realistic writer in this field, a new novel by this author is now on the stands."

$106,000 Blood Money was an undoubted winner. So great was the demand for more Hammett that Tower Books, an imprint of the World Publishing Company of Cleveland, Ohio, issued it as a hardback soon after, an extremely rare progression. Tower Books published inexpensive reprint editions that sold in J. C. Penney

Jonathan Press J17 July 6, 1945

for 49¢, twice the price of a digest paperback, but more visible to readers who didn't haunt newsstands. Dell Publishing, a mass-market paperback house, printed 170,000 copies as Dell 53, the first of its many reprints of the Mercury books. Both the Tower and Dell editions were titled simply *Blood Money*.

This experiment worked as well as *EQMM*, even though the material was frankly inferior. The two stories together were nowhere near novel length. The type and the leading were enlarged to bulk the text, generously estimated at 38,000 words, so that it fills a standard 128-page, 8 signature digest. In "The Big Knockover," a mastermind gathers the top crooks from across the country to simultaneously rob two banks of millions. Rather than the expected split, the crooks are mowed down so that only the mastermind would take away the loot. Hammett confirms 64 deaths, though a few others probably will die of their picturesque wounds. The soon-toexpire gangsters are mere tags with wild names: the Dis-and-Dat Kid, Rumdum Smith, Bluepoint Vance, Toby the Lugs. The survivors are paper characterizations meant to be filled in by casting directors. Only a beautifully written opening and the frenetic pace of close-up violence carry the reader through. Wildly overstuffed with so much plot that a more experienced writer would have taken the opportunity to slow it to full novel length—"$106,000 Blood Money" is an implausible appendage to the real story—Hammett had no such luxury. He'd taken a year off from *Black Mask* for advertising work that paid much better, but his health didn't even allow that. A new *Black Mask* editor, the now-famed Joseph Shaw, lured Hammett back with higher pay rates, a rope Hammett grabbed when he collapsed at the advertising office, coughing blood. His next project was a true novel, *Red Harvest*. After that short stories were trifles he didn't take seriously. "I'm one of the few—if there are any more—people moderately literate who take the detective story seriously . . . the detective story as a form. Some day somebody's going to make 'literature' out of it," he wrote Blanche Knopf in 1928. Hammett always deprecated his work, but he saw his novels as close to that "literature," not the short stories.

Others disagreed. Hammett's voice, pace, and violence were new to American fiction as well as to the mystery. Inferior early Hammett reverberated across Prohibition, Depression, and War as the legacy to larger-than-life frontier characters from Paul Bunyon to Davy Crockett. His stories were slices deep into the American psyche, painted with a minimum of words that bared the consequences of fury and desire that lay inside everyone, not merely professional crooks. (At least in those stories where he could afford to do characterization in place of pure action.) The increase in quality of writing in the remarkably short span from 1923, the first Op story, to 1930, when *The Maltese Falcon* sealed his fame, is astonishing. Readers saw it all and wanted more.

Buoyed by the reception, Dannay's pent-up enthusiasm exploded. Hammett couldn't be confined to the narrow confines of a single digest. Dannay proposed a trilogy, three volumes of Hammett shorts with all the editorial apparatus he brought to *EQMM*.

Spivak used Lillian Hellman as an intermediary. Hammett's long-term mistress, herself an acclaimed playwright often with Hammett editing and rewriting, Hellman had a stormy relationship with Hammett as novelistic as Scott and Zelda's. She acted as his literary representative while he was in the Army, although ironically at the time of *$106,000 Blood Money* he was stationed at Fort Monmouth, NJ, a stone's throw south of Brooklyn. (In WWI he never got out of Maryland.) Soon after he was transferred to Adak in the Aleutian Islands off Alaska, his permanent post. His letters to Hellman betray his ambivalence about the project. Spend the minimal amount of time on it; don't feel obligated to take lunch with Spivak, he wrote. Keep an eye on Dannay, "the Ellery Queen taste can be pretty bad at times."

Lee was by far the better writer of the pair, with an eventual clean, ironic style that better fit the post-Depression world. Dannay's editorial introductions were full of gush and cutesy, addicted to the puns and wordplay that at the end overwhelmed the Queen novels when they became the plot drivers. More positively, he knew everything about and everybody in the mystery world; his omniscience there matched that of the Queen character. When he focused on the history of the mystery he equaled Hammett in mastery of his field.

The Adventures of Sam Spade and Other Stories, Bestseller Mystery B50, appeared on April 14, 1944. The cover included the enticement, "Introduction by Ellery Queen." It's impossible to believe that Hellman spent even a moment editing Dannay's prose: the intro was classic Dannay: "Meet the rough, tough dick of *The Maltese Falcon*. Meet the man with a V-for-Victory face who looks like a blond satan... Meet the wild man from Frisco who always calls a spade a spade. Meet Sam." (If that's the after, what could the before have been like?) Hammett signed his early letters to Josephine, his wife, Sam. Sam Hammett became Dash Hammett after success as a writer; a piece of Sam always hid just under the surface. The two Sams became indistinguishable in the public mind after Humphrey Bogart made Sam Spade immortal. No matter that only three Spade short stories existed, "A Man Called Spade," "They Can Only Hang You Once," and "Too Many Have Lived," each written in 1932 and published the next year in respectable, non-pulpish, high-paying magazines, each throwaways well-written in his now slick style, each detective stories that could have come from the typewriters of

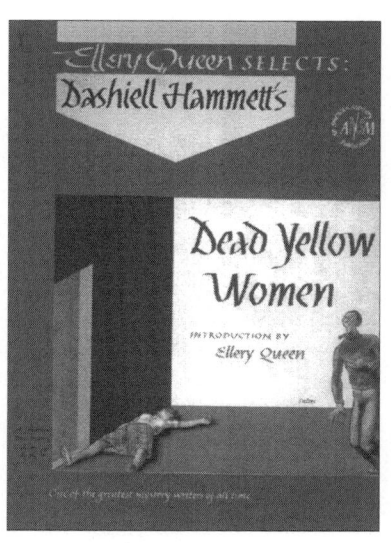

Jonathan Press J29 January 22, 1945

anyone in the business. Dannay had finally learned some business skills. He understood that in publishing you lead with your ace, just as he had when he put a Spade story first in the Table of Contents to Volume 1, Number 1 of *EQMM*. He filled out the back of the book to the needed 128 pages with four miscellaneous stories, including, naturally, "Nightshade," the story Hammett had written for the almost-never-seen *Mystery League*. The inevitable Dell edition, 90 left it out, along with "The Judge Laughed Last," a fun legal story with a great twist ending. "The Assistant Murderer," a private eye yarn, and "His Brother's Keeper," a solid character study of the seamy side of boxing, were kept. The print run was 202,000 copies.

The Continental Op and *The Return of the Continental Op* followed, on April 13 and July 6, 1945. Hammett had written 28 Op stories, many of them at novelette length. Dannay needed to be selective rather than pad these out. He pulled out four for the first, "Fly Paper," "Death on Pine Street," (originally "Women, Politics and Murder"), "Zigzags of Treachery," and "The Farewell Murder," and five for the second, "The Whosis Kid," "The Gutting of Couffignal," "Death and Company," "One Hour," and "The Tenth Clue" (originally "The Tenth Clew"). (American usage until the 1930s preferred the spelling "clew" over "clue".) Dell reprinted them whole as 129 and 154, with printings of 251,000 and 200,000 respectively.

Nobody ever grew rich from paperbacks. Their cover price of 25¢ needed to provide profits to the publisher, distributor, and seller and cover all printing costs and overhead along the way. That left a standard penny to be split as reprint fees to the original publisher and author. Hammett probably got to keep that penny for himself, minus whatever cut Dannay took as editor. Neither print runs nor sales figures are available for the Mercury books, but at $1000 per 100,000 copies, the total Hammett made for the first four, even with the Dell reprints thrown in, had to be less than he made in a month in Hollywood.

Hammett wasn't in Hollywood any more, of course. He took his age-related discharge from the Army and went back to Hellman, drinking heavily and suffering from emphysema in addition to his now 12-year-old case of writer's block. For a change he appreciated the mounds of praise Dannay had heaped on him and sent him a first edition of *The Maltese Falcon*, inscribed "For Fred Dannay, with all due thanks for his help in keeping this stuff from dying on the vine."

(The comparison is unfair, but one inscribed first of the *Falcon* is on AbeBooks, and it goes for $18,500.)

His resistance overcome, Hammett had no trouble acceding to a request to turn the trilogy into a longer series. "The first three volumes of Hammett shorts met with instant and popular approval," Dannay wrote in the introduction to *Hammett Homicides*. "Readers took pencil, pen, and typewriter in hand and shouted on paper: We want more Hammett short stories!" Bestseller Mystery B81, published December 20, 1946, featured four more Op stories, "The House in Turk Street," "The Girl with the Silver Eyes," "Night Shots," and "The Main Death," plus a pair of character studies, "Two Sharp Knives," and "Ruffian's Wife." Dell 223 included all six stories with a print run of 201,000. "Two Sharp Knives," was the second-to-last story Hammett published. It shows a quiet mastery that makes his subsequent silence all the more wrenching. "Night Shots," conversely, is an early story whose plot device is essentially identical to the Spade story "They Can Only Hang You Once." The device is no more plausible late than early, but the fact that Hammett could use it for both detectives, despite the supposed difference in their styles, shows that Hammett's take on the hardboiled school was often much closer to the standard story of deduction than most people remember. His yarns of over-the-top violence are worse stories but more fun as storytelling. That's an internal contradiction that always ate at him.

Dead Yellow Women, Jonathan Press J29, was published just a month later on January 22, 1947, and followed the same pattern. Four Op yarns, "Dead Yellow Women," "The Golden Horseshoe," "House Dick" ("Bodies Piled Up"), and "Who Killed Bob Teal?" were bulked out to 128 pages by "The Green Elephant" and "The Hairy One." The yellow women of the title story are all Chinese, a matter-of-fact reference to the language of 1925. Hammett actually satirizes the stereotyped imagery other authors used to scorn the Chinese and treats them little different from his other ethnics. From today's viewpoint that's not much of a virtue, since his Italians, Mexicans, Irish, Armenians, and the rest are mostly interchangeable foreign splashes of color rather than individuals. So are many of his Americans in the Op stories, but those are balanced by more respectable depictions seldom found in the immigrant ranks. "Who Killed Bob Teal?" is the only Op story not to appear in *Black Mask*. They flat out rejected it and Hammett found a home in a lesser pulp, *True Detective Stories*. A true detective story must be written by a true detective, no? The editors sneered at their witless readers and splashed the byline "Dashiell Hammett of the Continental Detective Agency" across the page. Perhaps suspecting that readers might find these stories lesser Hammett, Dell 308 had a print run of only 175,000.

Dead Yellow Women was also billed as an Ellery Queen Selects collection, appearing close after Palmer and Stout. The title page hammered home Dannay's contributions: "Selected and Edited with Introduction and Critical Notes by Ellery Queen." The copyright page goes even further. "This book was selected for

Mercury Mystery #120 February 10, 1948

us by Ellery Queen, famous for his bestselling books, movies, and radio shows. Mr. Queen is also editor of *Ellery Queen's Mystery Magazine*. These mysteries are sometimes reprinted in full, but more often they are cut to speed up the story—always, of course, with the permission of the author or his publisher. These stories have not been cut."

Abridgement was the norm for paperback reprints. The standard length of novels varies by decade; the thirties happened to be a time when novels grew longer. Even mysteries often swelled to over 300 pages. Paperbacks had the disadvantage—for the publishers—of being sold at a fixed price. Increasing the length of a digest by even one full 16-page signature meant an 8% increase in paper costs. Spivak's people played with the font and leading sizes but those had limits. Editors went through manuscripts to cut out every spare clause and page of atmospherics that didn't affect the plot.

Dannay did not abridge his

Jonathan Press J36 September 21, 1948

pet series stories. He did edit them lightly, usually changing a word or cutting a phrase for mainly inexplicable reasons. Terry Zobeck, a collector of original Hammett magazine appearances, did the yeoman's work of comparing the originals with the digest Hammetts word-by-word in a long series of posts on Don Herron's *Up and Down These Mean Streets* blog (www.donherron.com). Zobeck's examination of "Who Killed Bob Teal" reveals that Dannay frequently cut the ending of a sentence. "Finally she shrugged, her face cleared, and she looked up at us." became "Finally she shrugged, her face cleared." "Dean and I rode down in the elevator in silence, and walked out into Gough Street." became "Dean and I rode down in the elevator." In all, 155 words were deleted, about 2% of the total wordage.

Every story that Zobeck did comparisons on has these changes, some more, some less. Dannay seldom changed words, although he sometimes changed names: Jacob Coplin for Frank Toplin; George Street for Turk Street. Once or twice he softened a word for more modern sensibilities, as when he changed "nigger-wool tobacco" to "black tobacco." Most of these stories had appeared in *EQMM* before being collected in the digests, so space issues might have been a factor there. There is an art to getting stories to fit at the bottom of a page and not slop over a paragraph when the type size is fixed. Zobeck also notes that we can't be sure that Dannay had his hands on original magazines for every story. Some had been syndicated in newspapers during the 30s, a time when newspapers frequently ran fiction in their pages. If those were what Dannay had to work with then unknown editors could have made the changes for their own arcane reasons.

The recent Library of America release of *Dashiell Hammett: Crime Stories and Other Writings*, containing two dozen Hammett works, does go back to the originals for their texts. True obsessives may prefer them but ordinary readers should find the changes invisible.

With no signs of the demand for Hammett abating, Dannay bowed to readers in his usual style. "You begged, requisitioned, commanded—all but subpoenaed another collection of Hammett tales; you would take no denial." *Nightmare Town* appeared as Mercury Mystery #120, published February 10, 1948. The Ellery Queen Selects banner was gone, never to return. "Nightmare Town" was a corruption that prefigured Poisonville in *Red Harvest*, "The Scorched Face" and "Corkscrew" were action-laden adventures of the Op. "Albert Pastor at Home" was a short short that had appeared in *Esquire* in 1933, a sign of Hammett's longing for literary recognition. Dell 377 followed with a print run of 277,000, though this was more an indication of the times since it's in line with their other contemporaneous titles. Dell 382, *Celeste The Gold Coast Virgin*, a historical romance by Rosamond Marshall, towered over every other title with a printing of 412,000.

Spivak may have thought six titles was really, truly all there would be because he filled in the next two years with reissues, starting from the beginning. *$106,000 Blood Money* appeared as *The Big Knockover*, Jonathan Press J36, published September 21, 1948; *The Adventures of Sam Spade and Other Stories* became *They Can Only Hang You Once and Other Stories*, Mercury Mystery #131, published January 4, 1949; *The Continental Op* retained its title when reissued as Jonathan Press J40, also in 1949. They are reissues rather than reprints in the sense that the contents were completely reset with new type and pagination even though the 128-page length remained inviolate.

Then, in 1950, a blockbuster announcement. Spivak would publish *three* more books of Hammett shorts, one that year, one each of the next two, essentially cleaning out Hammett's entire inventory except for a very few minor stories. All would have the Queen introductions and apparatus.

The Creeping Siamese, Jonathan Press J48, was published September 22, 1950. "The Creeping Siamese" and "Tom, Dick or Harry" ("Mike, Alec or Rufus?") were Op stories, "This King Business" was the longest non-novel Hammett wrote, "The

Jonathan Press J40 1949

Man Who Killed Dan Odams," "The Joke on Eloise Morey," and "The Nails in Mr. Cayterer," that last having the creepiest title of any Hammett story, filled out the volume. *Woman in the Dark*, Jonathan Press J59, followed on July 18, 1951. It contained seven stories, six of them minor ones from Hammett's earliest days—"Arson Plus," "The Girl with Silver Eyes," "The Black Hat That Wasn't There," ("It"), "Afraid of a Gun," "Holiday, and "The Man Who Stood In the Way" ("The Vicious Circle")—plus the title story "Woman in the Dark," published as a three-part serial in *Liberty* in 1933, a pure character study that pressed the case, as Hammett's work often did, that the low lives had far better morals and standards than the upper crust. In two years Hammett would be partying with the swells full time, perhaps another hint why he no longer could write that sort of story, or any other. "Arson Plus" was the very first Op story, from the October 1, 1923 *Black Mask*,

Jonathan Press J48 September 22, 1950

so early that it had appeared under the pseudonym Hammett was still using, Peter Collinson. It's a standard mystery featuring deduction rather than fisticuffs; with a small amount of rewriting it wouldn't surprise anyone by appearing under the Queen name. "The Vicious Circle" was also published as by Collinson. *The Creeping Siamese*, Dell 538, had a fine print run of 305,000 but *Woman in the Dark*, which perhaps tellingly would have come out in 1952, never appeared.

That left *A Man Named Thin*, announced for 1952. Hammett fans not *au courant* with *EQMM* must have been puzzled by the name. No story with that title existed. In the novel titled *The Thin Man*, the title character is the murder victim. The detective is famously Nick Charles. It's true that the movies conflated the two for the titles of Thin Man sequels, but it's impossible to imagine Hammett doing so.

The answer lies in the story "The Nails in Mr. Cayterer." Hammett introduced a parody of his hardboiled detectives named Robin Thin. A foppish poet, a character says of him, "I never saw [a detective] that looked, acted, or talked less like one." This story was published in *Black Mask* in 1926, a fact that should shake modern notions of it being exclusively dedicated to hardboiled tough guys. The averaged-sized Thin was in contrast to his detective agency owning father "Big" Thin and of course to the overweight Op. Hammett was thin—his nickname in WWI had been Slim and that was before tuberculosis periodically dropped his weight into the 120s, frightening on his 6'1" frame—and also Thin— Hammett worshipped literature and would spend his career trying for literary glory. There's no question that Thin lived in the same world as the Op: the name of the Dis-and-Dat Kid later seen in "The Big Knockover" is dropped on the first page. Hammett must have liked the Thin character because he wrote a second story about him, apparently titled "The Figure of Incongruity," which got sold to some detective magazine that went out of business before it could be published. No sane editor would publish a detective story titled "The Figure of Incongruity" in 1926 or elsewhen. Dannay's punning instincts took over. On the analogy of the Sam Spade tale, "A Man Named Spade," he dubbed it "A Man Named Thin." Let the uncertainty in readers' minds make the truth all the better when it appeared.

The good will that Hammett had for Dannay is nowhere better in evidence than the fact that Hammett sold Dannay the exclusive rights to publish this story, this one "new" story from the author who hadn't published in over a decade. Dannay triumphantly announced it. In the Foreword to his 1946 anthology *To the Queen's Taste*, a sequel to *101 Years' Entertainment*, he bragged, "[I]f this unpublished story is made available to the public, it can only be through the pages of *Ellery Queen's Mystery Magazine*."

So true. *EQMM* didn't publish it and no Hammett anthology was published in 1952 or for the rest of the 1950s. The story languished, tantalizingly. Why Dannay didn't immediately publish "A Man Named Thin," playing another ace, is a deep mystery. Perhaps he thought it would work better to close out the Hammett series with the publicity of a newly-found work. That decision worked against him and Hammett. 1951 was the year that Hammett went to jail for contempt of court for taking the Fifth Amendment in a hearing before a federal District Court. Hammett became a publishing pariah then and even more so when he was blacklisted in 1953 after refusing to cooperate with the House Un-American Activities Committee.

Hammett spent the rest of the '50s broke and in ever poorer health. His fatal cancer was withheld from him but he quickly succumbed and died on January 8, 1961. Dannay used the occasion of the magazine's 20th anniversary to run his long-held file story in the March 1961 *EQMM*. Magazines have long lead dates and the story's introduction makes clear that Dannay thought Hammett was still alive at the time. (Why is March the anniversary month when the first issue was Fall 1941? I can't say and it's inconsistent with the 10th Anniversary issue

Black Mask joins *Ellery Queen* May 1953

being April 1951, that also featured a Hammett reprint, and contained a poll naming Hammett one of the 12 best mystery writers of all time.) Hopefully because of a collector's sense of uniformity, Dannay had his publisher, Joseph W. Ferman, revive the Mercury Mystery line to publish it in 1962 in digest format as Mercury #233. (The last Mercury Mystery was #209. The numbering continued with the bizarrely-named *Mercury Mystery-Book Magazine* though #226 and then the more sensible *Mercury Mystery Magazine* through #232 in 1959.) Dannay's *EQMM* intro is reprinted in full, not updated to acknowledge Hammett's death, although a black-bordered Postscript informs all readers who hadn't heard of his demise. Seven other stories, all early minor works, joined the title story: "Wages of Crime" ("The Sardonic Star of Tom Doody" as by Peter Collinson), "The Gatewood Caper" ("Crooked Souls"), "The Barber and His Wife" (as by Peter Collinson), "Itchy the Debonair"

Mercury Mystery #233 February 20, 1962

("Itchy"), "The Second-Story Angel," "In the Morgue" ("The Dimple"), and "When Luck's Running Good" ("Laughing Masks"). "The Gatewood Caper" was an Op story, making 27 of the 28 Op stories available in the series. Only the second Op story, "Slippery Fingers" (also as by Peter Collinson), was excluded. Although it's considered the worst of the series and made use of fingerprint evidence dubious even in 1923, no good reason can be given for annoying completists by its absence.

Hammett's work saw a renaissance with his death. Pocket Books published several novels in 1962, Random House published *The Big Knockover*, a major collection of his longer short stories, plus the unfinished novel fragment "Tulip," in hardcover in 1966, and then came the inexorable archeology of finding every lost and unpublished story and putting them into covers, a project finally finished in 2014.

Today the Hammett digests are prime collectibles, seldom available in very good or better condition, probably why an online listing has all ten originals plus two of the reprints, an "excellent" set, for a mere $5000. Some diligent searching through bookfinder.com will produce nearly equal individual copies for less than $1000, including thirteen sets of postage.

Ironically, though *EQMM* has never faltered as the leading mystery magazine, Hammett's name is now far more potent than the authorial Queen, who is mostly out of print. That's due almost entirely to Hammett's novels, reinforced by the iconic movie versions: the shorter works are secondary in every sense. Hammett remains a touchstone of untamed American life, drawn with dispassion, yet acuteness, by a man of the same civilized wildness as his detectives. He, like Nick Charles, tried to put that rough first half of his life behind him yet in the end took pleasure in having old compatriots remind him of those good times. Thanks to Dannay, Hammett's shorts were brought back to life and served him well in the wilderness years. No glossy thick hardback reprints can match the feel of raw Hammett in the magical subliterariness of these digests.

↙ ↙

The past is **Steve Carper's** future. He created the Flying Cars and Food Pill website: flyingcarsandfoodpills.com to bring the past future of technological marvels back into life. A long-term collector of digests, other paperbacks, mystery and science fiction and about 10,000 other books, he's writing a new history and bibliography of the seminal f&sf publisher Gnome Press (gromepress.com). A collection of his own published science fiction, *Tyrannosaur Faire*, is available in paper and electronic format.

Dashiell Hammett Digest Bibliography
Content and Reprint Sources

$106,000 Blood Money Bestseller Mystery B40, June 15, 1943; reissued as **The Big Knockover** Jonathan Press J36, September 21, 1948.
• "The Big Knockover" (*Black Mask*, February 1927), Op
• "$106,000 Blood Money" (*Black Mask*, May 1927), Op

The Adventures of Sam Spade and Other Stories edited by Ellery Queen. Bestseller Mystery B50, April 14, 1944; reissued as **They Can Only Hang You Once and Other Stories** Mercury Mystery #131, January 4, 1949.
• "Too Many Have Lived" (*American Magazine*, October 1932), Spade
• "They Can Only Hang You Once" (*Collier's*, November 19, 1932), Spade
• "A Man Called Spade" (*American Magazine*, July 1932), Spade
• "The Assistant Murderer" (*Black Mask*, February 1926)
• "Nightshade" (*Mystery League Magazine*, October 1, 1933 as "Night Shade")
• "The Judge Laughed Last" (*Black Mask*, February 15, 1924 as "The New Racket")
• "His Brother's Keeper" (*Collier's*, February 17, 1934)

The Continental Op edited by Ellery Queen. Bestseller Mystery B62, April 13, 1945; reissued as Jonathan Press J40, 1949.
• "Fly Paper" (*Black Mask*, August 1929), Op
• "Death on Pine Street") (*Black Mask*, September 1924 as "Women, Politics and Murder"), Op
• "Zigzags of Treachery" (*Black Mask*, March 1, 1924), Op
• "The Farewell Murder" (*Black Mask*, February 1930), Op

The Return of the Continental Op edited by Ellery Queen. Jonathan Press J17, July 6, 1945.
• "The Whosis Kid" (*Black Mask*, March 1925), Op
• "The Gutting of Couffignal" (*Black Mask*, December 1925), Op
• "Death and Company" (*Black Mask*, November 1930), Op
• "One Hour" (*Black Mask*, April 1, 1924), Op
• "The Tenth Clue" (*Black Mask*, January 1, 1924 as "The Tenth Clew"), Op

Hammett Homicides edited by
Ellery Queen. Bestseller Mystery B81, December 20, 1946.
- "The House in Turk Street"
(*Black Mask*, April 15, 1924), Op
- "The Girl with the Silver Eyes"
(*Black Mask*, June 1924), Op
- "Night Shots"
(*Black Mask*, February 1, 1924), Op
- "The Main Death"
(*Black Mask*, June 1927), Op
- "Two Sharp Knives"
(*Collier's*, January 13, 1934)
- "Ruffian's Wife"
(*Sunset Magazine*, October 1925)

Dead Yellow Women edited by
Ellery Queen. Jonathan Press J29, January 22, 1947.
- "Dead Yellow Women"
(*Black Mask*, November 1925), Op
- "The Golden Horseshoe"
(*Black Mask*, November 1924), Op
- "House Dick"
(*Black Mask*, December 1, 1923 as "Bodies Piled Up"), Op
- "Who Killed Bob Teal?"
(*True Detective Stories*, Nov.1924), Op
- "The Green Elephant"
(*The Smart Set*, October 1923)
- "The Hairy One"
(*Sunset Magazine*, March 1925 as "Ber-Bulu")

Nightmare Town edited by Ellery Queen. Mercury Mystery #120, February 10, 1948.
- "Nightmare Town"
(*Argosy All-Story Weekly*, December 27, 1924), Op
- "The Scorched Face"
(*Black Mask*, May 1925), Op
- "Albert Pastor at Home"
(*Esquire*, Autumn 1933)
- "Corkscrew"
(*Black Mask*, September 1925)

The Creeping Siamese edited by
Ellery Queen. Jonathan Press J48, September 22, 1950.
- "The Creeping Siamese"
(*Black Mask*, March 1926), Op
- "The Man Who Killed Dan Odams"
(*Black Mask*, January 15, 1924)
- "The Nails in Mr. Cayterer"
(*Black Mask*, January 1926), Thin
- "The Joke on Eloise Morey"
(*Brief Stories*, June 1923)
- "Tom, Dick or Harry"
(*Black Mask*, January, 1925 as "Mike, Alec or Rufus?"), Op
- "This King Business"
(*Mystery Stories*, January 1928)

Woman In the Dark edited by
Ellery Queen. Jonathan Press J59, July 18, 1951.
- "Arson Plus"
(*Black Mask*, October 1, 1923 as by Peter Collinson), Op
- "The Girl with Silver Eyes"
(*Black Mask*, June 1924), Op
- "The Black Hat That Wasn't There"
(*Black Mask*, November 1923 as "It"), Op
- "Woman in the Dark"
(*Liberty* magazine, April 8, 1933, April 15, 1933, & April 22, 1933)
- "Afraid of a Gun"
(*Black Mask*, March 1, 1924)
- "Holiday"
(*The New Pearson's*, July 1923)
- "The Man Who Stood In the Way"
(*Black Mask*, June 15, 1923 as "The Vicious Circle" as by Peter Collinson)

A Man Named Thin edited by Ellery Queen. Mercury Mystery #233, February 20, 1962.
- "A Man Named Thin"
(*Ellery Queen's Mystery Magazine*, March 1961), Thin
- "Wages of Crime"
(*Brief Stories*, February 1923 as "The Sardonic Star of Tom Doody" as by Peter Collinson)
- "The Gatewood Caper"
(*Black Mask*, October 15, 1923 as "Crooked Souls"), Op
- "The Barber and His Wife"
(*Brief Stories*, December 1922 as by Peter Collinson)
- "Itchy the Debonair"
(*Brief Stories*, January 1924 as "Itchy")
- "The Second-Story Angel"
(*Black Mask*, November 15, 1923)
- "In the Morgue"
(*Saucy Stories*, October 15, 1923 as "The Dimple")
- "When Luck's Running Good"
(*Action Stories*, November 1923 as "Laughing Masks")

Paperback Parade #89
Review by Richard Krauss

"In *The Bone is Pointed*, the sixth book in the series, the reader sees the procedure required to perform the aboriginal black magic, 'pointing the bone,' a normally fatal activity."

It's always a pleasure to see the new edition of Gary Lovisi's *Paperback Parade* in your mailbox. His years of experience and knowledge of classic paperback originals fuels his own articles and his extended network of experts and collectors who contribute immeasurably to the mix.

The issue begins with Lovisi's far-ranging "Paperback Talk," that combines news, excerpts from readers' letters of comment, background on featured articles, remembrances of bookpeople who have recently passed, and interesting bits of paperback history and trivia. His friendly reportage creates an inviting entry into the heart of the in-depth articles to follow.

The first of those spotlights Arthur Upfield's series featuring half-aboriginal Detective Inspector Napoleon Bonaparte, or "Bony," as he's most often referred to, by Philip K. Jones. Upfield moved to Australia early on and wrote 29 novels about his character. Well known on newsstands down under, but far more obscure in other geos, Jones traces the series from start to finish with commentary, synopses and loads of cover repros. I couldn't help thinking of the similarity with Tony Hillerman's series—a continental native joins local law enforcement where he uses his training and knowledge of native culture in murder investigations. Fortunately, today these novels are far easier to sample and collect outside Australia, than when they were written.

You might say *Paperback Parade*'s mission is to celebrate the diversity of paperback originals—the well-known, the obscure, the famous and infamous. Not every article will strike a chord with every reader, but collectively they broaden our exposure and knowledge of this low-cost literary mainstay, and every article includes at least a few fascinating tidbits.

Cases in point, Gary Lovisi's report on Hustler Paperbacks and Michael S. Smith's on "nurse romance." In the space of four years (1979–1982) Hustler pumped out ~200 paperback books. Lovisi marks it the end of "The Last Gasp of Sleaze." Their covers were suggestive but nothing beyond the cover art of earlier racy PBOs—but the stories between the covers replaced titillating innuendo with explicit sex—hard core porn. And fair warning, there are a few excerpts included that leave nothing to the imagination. Hustler tapped a full range of genres including science fiction, fantasy, crime, horror, western, sports and gothic to appeal to the widest audience. But even Lovisi has reservations, "While I feel the books are readable, that doesn't mean I want to read them . . ."

Like every article in *PP*, this one includes a generous selection of cover images. Hustler used both painted and photographic images—all with nearly nude women. The article wraps with a complete checklist of all ~200 titles, that runs nine pages, compiled by Dan Roberts and Chris Eckhoff.

Michael S. Smith's piece on Ace nurse romance novels traces their evolution from "nurse"—one of a handful of key occupations for women prior to the women's liberation movement—to the "medical romance" of more contemporary times. It was a big market and Smith offers a few surprises (to me at least) on the writers and artists who were part of it. He also provides an eight page checklist of Ace's full library.

PP designer, Richard Greene contributes another "Matchless Paperbacks" column. This one is about *The Fifth Estate* by Robin Moore, who also wrote *The French Connection*, *The Green Berets*, *The Crippled Eagles*, and surprisingly *The Happy Hooker*, with Xaviera Hollander and Yvonne Dunleavy.

Gary Lovisi's article "Short-Run Series: Checkerbooks" was my favorite of the issue. A line of only twelve books, Lovisi covers the details of its origin, marketplace failure and a synopsis of each volume, along with cover images. What a great, diverse series it was! One of its most collectable titles, "Lady, Mind that Corpse," is featured on the cover of this edition of *Paperback Parade*.

Finally, long-time PBO collector, Fred Cropper lists "10 of the Greatest Writers of Paperback Originals." His list is illustrated by cover images and photographs of several of his "greats" along with what turns out to be 15 writers—because there were so many greats.

Paperback Parade is a real favorite of mine. I look forward to every edition. Individually, they provide several worthwhile hours of entertainment and education—and they remain excellent sources of reference. When you think of several issues collectively, the title is simply indispensable.

A three-issue subscription to *Paperback Parade* is $40 (US), $65 (other countries).

Select back issues are available for $15 each plus $3 for postage and handling (US), see website for other countries.

Gryphon Books
PO Box 280209
Brooklyn, NY 11228
gryphonbooks.com

"Mr. UFO"
Timothy Green Beckley's Paranormal Odyssey
Profile by Tom Brinkmann

The Beginning . . .

Timothy Green Beckley started his paranormal odyssey in New Brunswick, New Jersey in 1947, growing up in a house that was haunted. By the age of ten, in 1957, he had his first of three UFO sightings; no wonder Tim was intrigued when he saw an issue of *Fate* magazine on the newsstand and purchased it that same year. *Fate*'s original publisher had been Ray Palmer who had started the digest in March 1948. In 1953 Palmer had sold his interests in *Fate* to Curtis and Mary Fuller and went on to publish numerous digests and magazines with titles such as *Mystic Magazine*, *Other Worlds*, *Flying Saucers*, *The Hidden World*, *Search Magazine*, *Space World*, and others.

Meanwhile, at the age of fourteen, Tim had purchased

Timothy Green Beckley circa 1978. Photo by Jeff Goodman.

his own mimeograph machine and had started a UFO newsletter which he titled *Interplanetary News Service Report*. At about that time, Tim had placed a personal ad in the September 1961 issue of Palmer's, then digest-sized, *Flying Saucers* magazine stating, "WANTED: flying saucer magazines, books or bulletins. Also anything on the strange or supernatural." In the November 1962 issue of *Flying Saucers*, Tim placed another personal ad that read:

"The INTERPLANETARY NEWS SERVICE REPORT is issuing a drive to secure data relating to the saucer enigma. This data may be in the form of photos, news

Flying Saucers September 1961 with Tim's first personal ad.

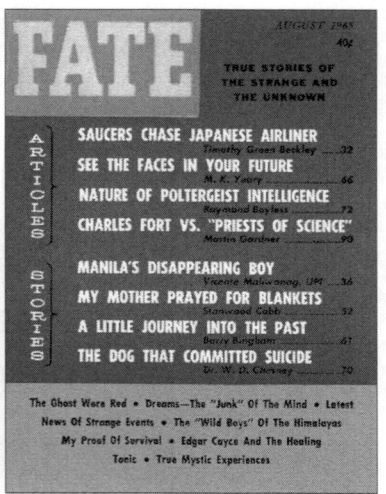

Fate August 1965

clippings, sightings, pamphlets, bulletins, or magazines. We are also interested in publishing special reports, written by the readers of *Flying Saucers*. These reports will be sold to the general public."

Tim was off and running and, hasn't stopped since.

... And Beyond

Tim says of the digest format, "[The] digest was never a popular type of magazine as far as distributors and retailers went. They hated the size 'cause it would get lost. There were few racks that size."

Timothy Green Beckley's earliest article for *Fate* magazine, as far as he remembers and, from what I can figure out through looking on eBay, was in the August 1965 issue (volume 18, #8, issue 185). The digest was still owned by the Fullers, Curtis as publisher and wife Mary as editor. The article, titled "Saucers Chase Japanese Airliner," was a short piece concerning a Convair 240 airliner carrying 28 passengers that had been followed by a UFO for over 55 miles and then the UFO disappeared. Also, included in the piece was a reproduced article about the incident from the March 27, 1965 edition of *Pacific Stars and Stripes* a U. S. Armed Forces newspaper. Tim had gotten his foot in the door of *Fate*.

In an email to the author on March 15, 2015, Tim wrote, "Outside of *Fate* none of these pubs sold very well. *Fate* did a respectable 40,000 on the newsstand—they had about a hundred-thousand subscribers but that nearly ruined them 'cause they would get paid like a buck a subscription from Publishers Clearing House and other discount outlets and little by little the postage went up and the advertising revenue went way down."

Fate's October 1966 issue (volume 19, #10, issue 199) had another article by Tim and co-author E. J. Babcock, titled "UFO Plagues N. J. Reservoir." This concerned a much witnessed and well covered UFO sighting in northern New Jersey that

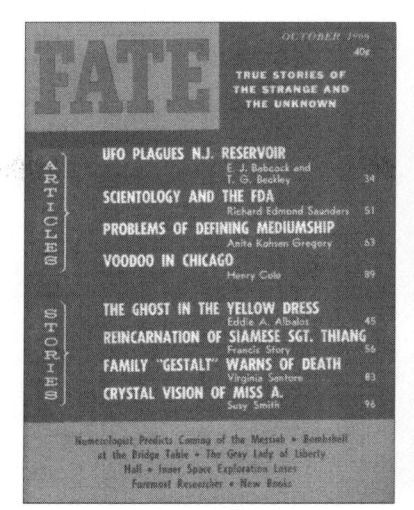

Fate October 1966

Fate April 1970

took place on the cold, clear night of January 11, 1966, in Tim's backyard so to speak. The man-made Wanaque Resevoir is over six-and-a-half miles long and one mile wide. It starts, at its northern most point, a few miles south of the New York state line; thirty-two miles northwest of New York City. The sightings of the UFO/s started at 6:20 PM over Ringwood, N. J. as it headed south, "like the devil." The object was described variously as "a white garishly bright disc two feet in diameter;" "a big glowing white mass;" "a continous light that changed from white to red to green and back to white;" and was apparently shape-shifting from a disc to cigar-shaped. The local police stations and radio stations "lit up" with hundreds of calls from concerned witnesses. The witnesses ranged the gamut from citizens to police officers, reservoir security guards, a priest, a Civil Defense Director, the Mayor of Wanaque, and so on. It was also observed melting a hole "about 40 to 50 feet in diameter" in the ice-covered reservoir with a beam of light. The UFO was sighted all over northern New Jersey that night until it disappeared around 9 p.m. There were other UFO sightings around the Wanaque Reservoir over the next eighteen months. The U. S. Air Force confiscated all the photos they could, including some taken by police officers, but they missed a few photos which were published in various papers and the second issue of Dell's 1967 *Flying Saucers UFO Reports* magazine. Tim's article in *Fate* was one of the earliest published in a national magazine. And, the May 1967 issue of *Science & Mechanics* even had the "Exclusive" cover story, "America's Most Awsome UFO Mystery—The Wanaque, N. J. Sightings: On-the-scene reports from 24 eye-witnesses."

Through the years, Tim has had many articles published in *Fate*, such as, "A New Look at Old Monsters" (3/69), "Russia Searches For the Abominable Snowman"

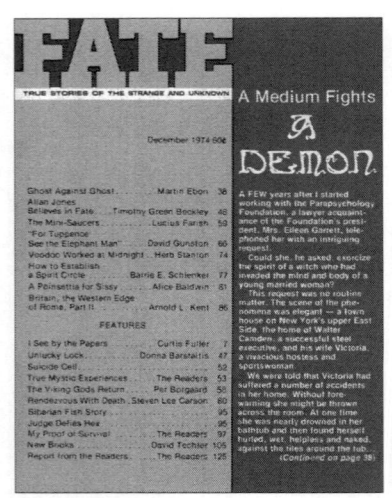

Fate December 1974

Fate February 1975

(4/70); "Allan Jones Believes In Fate" (12/74); "[Ernest] Borgnine Believes He Has Lived Before" (2/75); and "On the Trail of the Oracle of Delphi" (7/06). I'm sure there are many others, but these are the ones I have been able to find.

Ray Palmer's *Flying Saucers* magazine had originally been titled *Other Worlds Science Stories*, which was a fiction digest. In 1957, Palmer changed its title to *Flying Saucers from Other Worlds* and alternated all-fiction issues with non-fiction issues. In 1959, it became *Flying Saucers* with the subtitle, "The Magazine of Space Conquest," and was all non-fiction. It had become an 8.5 x 11 inch magazine by 1966, when Tim was writing a column for it, called "On the Trail of the Flying Saucers," in exchange for advertising space for "Flying Saucer Books, Magazines and Records by All Authors and From All Publishers." Tim's column ran semi-regularly in *Flying Saucers* thoughout the late sixties and into 1970. Seven of Tim's columns were reprinted in his book *Strange Saga* (2013).

The bulletin/magazine *Saucer News* started in 1954 and was edited by James Moseley and, eventually, Gray Barker. In 1967, the then twenty-year-old Tim was listed as "Managing Editor & Advertising Manager," and had written some book reviews as well (Fall 1967, volume 14, #3). Both Gray Barker and John Keel were contributing editors for *Saucer News*. Tim's first book, *The Shaver Mystery and the Inner Earth* (1967), was published by Gray Barker's West Virginia-based Saucerian Press, as was his second, *Book of Space Brothers* (1969). I don't have the space in this article to go into the careers of Jim Moseley and Gray Barker, who were both noted and influential UFO/paranormal investigators, authors, and friends of Tim's. But, for the interested, they both have Wikipedia pages.

In 1968 Tim had his article, "UFOs Use High-Tension Lines for Re-Charging," published in the third issue of *Beyond* (November 1968). But, because of limited space here, the *Beyond* article I want to focus on is from its ninth issue, May 1969, titled "Red-Eyed Winged Creature Terrorizes W. Virginia Town." The article concerns the genesis of the Mothman legend; on November 15, 1966 in Point Pleasant, West Virginia, on a "lover's lane" that was the overgrown driveway leading to the parking lot of a closed, run-down factory which had produced TNT during WWII. That night, two young married couples, riding in the same car, had the first encounter with what would later become known as Mothman. At first they thought the "red eyes" were the tail-lights of a car in front of them until their headlights revealed the gray, eight-foot tall, winged-creature with "huge, bright red eyes." As they turned the car around to flee the area, they saw the creature head towards the abandoned factory. Then, they heard a noise like a "large squeaking mouse," at the same time they noticed the shadow of a large winged-creature on the road ahead, keeping up with the car. It followed them all the way back to the town but, seemed to turn back toward the factory, being repelled by Point Pleasant's lights. The two couples drove directly to the police station to report what they had just experienced. Deputy Halstead listened to the story and drove back to the scene with the two spooked couples to see what there was to see, which was nothing. But, the radio in the Deputy's car went wacky, broadcasting what sounded like a fast playing record of some kind. Deputy Halstead believed the couples had seen something, but told *Beyond*, i.e., Tim Beckley, that he discounted the theory of a

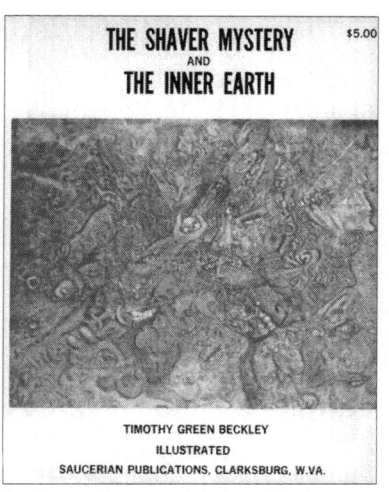

The Shaver Mystery and the Inner Earth published in 1967

local who suggested it was a large Sand Hill Crane flying overhead.

The hub-bub increased: nearby, a TV signal went wacky and emitted a "weird humming" sound; a dog chased after something with "red eyes" into a field and, disappeared forever; a daytime sighting of the creature rising up from a field, then it followed a car traveling 70 mph; the creature was seen standing on the edge of a golf course; five people spotted it flying over the airport, and so on.

On December 7, 1966, John Keel, Fortean researcher, "author, globe-trotting reporter, TV scriptwriter," and friend of Tim's, visited Point Pleasant and interviewed a dozen witnesses who had seen Mothman. Keel reported to *Beyond*/Tim that, "Sincere testimony of all the witnesses would seem to place the burden of proof onto the shoulders of the disbelievers." One night, Keel visited the abandoned TNT factory with some of the witnesses, who were afraid to accompany him in at first.

Search Magazine January 1970

Artwork for Tim's column, "World of the Off Beat" that appeared in *Search Magazine* January 1970

Eventually, a teenage girl, who had seen Mothman, and her boyfriend decided to go in with Keel. They saw nothing, at first. Then the girl went into a hysterical panic claiming when she looked back at a doorway they had just passed through she had seen the creature. Keel saw nothing except her reaction. Then, the witnesses outside began yelling that they had just seen Mothman running through a field but, Keel still saw nothing, even when he looked for tracks with his flashlight. Then, there was a "high pitched whine" which caused a witness to bleed from an ear for an hour.

The UFO sightings started that morning around the Ohio and Kanawha Rivers, which were only a mile from the TNT factory and, continued for months. One sighting involved the Mothman coming out of a UFO, flying over the factory and reentering the saucer. The whole thing seemed to culminate on December 15, 1967 when the Silver Bridge, which spanned the Ohio River, connecting West Virginia to Ohio, collapsed, killing fifty-four people including a few of the Mothman/UFO witnesses. Various explanations of the Mothman phenomena were proposed by locals, some of whom were witnesses, and John Keel, that ranged from a prehistoric bird that had survived by living in undergound caves to a "robot controlled UFOnaut." Tim visited the town and site of the bridge collapse and learned of thirteen UFO sightings within an hour before its collapse; in other words, he did the footwork and some interviews while there. Keel eventually wrote his book on the phenomena, *The Mothman Prophecies* (1975) which was turned into the movie of the same name starring Richard Gere in 2002.

Search Magazine was another Ray Palmer digest devoted to the paranormal which had started as *Mystic Magazine* in 1953, after Palmer had left *Fate*. In *Search*, issue #89, dated January 1970, Palmer's editorial compared a map of the

Artwork for Tim's column, "World of the Off Beat" from *Search Magazine* January 1971

continent of "Pan," commonly refered to as Lemuria, which had been published in the book *Oahspe* by John Ballou Newbrough in 1881, with an undersea map of the Pacific Ocean that had recently been published in *The National Geographic*, October 1969. Both maps were included in the editorial and, the comparison was startling in their simularity. Palmer then explained the issue's cover photo, that of a baby girl named Vickey, who was the daughter of Palmer's niece which had no article connected to it inside. Palmer explained this was his way of showing his love of family and his hope that the world would be a better place for future generations.

Tim had a column in the same issue called, "World of the Off Beat," that had a cover blurb announcing it. Tim's column concerned various predictions by different psychics, the first of which was Paul Twitchell head of ECKANKAR "the science of Soul Travel," who predicted, in an interview, that humans landing on the moon would result in "The Moon Plague," a virus that would be brought back to earth by those who traveled there. Twitchell claimed this virus would equal that of the Black Plague of the Dark Ages and, that "a quarter of the human race" would die from it before it could be brought under control and stopped. Tim mentions that according to the people who keep score, Twitchell's predictions were 85% correct. The "Moon Plague" prediction belonged to the 15% that didn't pan out. Twitchell's method of "soul travel," i.e., Astral Projection, or leaving one's body, to read the "Akashic Records" which were described as an astral deck of cards that each individual had that could be read on the astral plane; each card representing a significant event in a past life.

Next, were a variety of psychic's views of what would become of California and the East Coast in the near or distant future and how World War III might come about. The seers included Jean Dixon, Daniel Logan, Edgar Cayce, Ted Owens, and others. Dixon thought that California would eventually sink into the ocean, but within the next fifty years, not in April 1969, as she had been misquoted as saying.

Search Magazine May 1970

She also felt that Atlantis would rise again "within moments" of California sinking. Cayce also believed that Atlantis would rise again before the year 2000. And, Ted Owens thought that WW III would be fought with germs, not atomic weapons.

Search's May 1970 issue (#91) had a cover with a line drawing of a variety of flowers whose colors made it look sort of psychedelic. The flowery cover art combined with the chosen cover blurbs, "Love Makes the World Go Round," "The Zodiac 'Pill,'" and "Are Marriages Made In Heaven?" set the tone for the issue. In a classic editorial, Palmer humorously pointed out the hypocricy and irony of the Bible's version of the creation of Eve to cure Adam's loneliness, and he ended up writing about the emancipation of women and test-tube babies!

Tim's "World of the Off Beat" column covered "Reincarnation— Your Past Lives." The article started with the Rev. Noel Street, a psychic from New Zealand, who was also a reincarnation expert who gave a talk and demonstration of his ability to ascertain people's past lives at a parapsychology seminar held by Jim Moseley in New York City. Rev. Street picked people from the audience and meditated, then told them about their past lives. Rev. Street explained that we have all lived many lives "in accordance with our ability to work out our Karma." To explain how Rev. Street can see people's past lives, again, the Akashic Records, here likened to "stepping stones of our lives, which meander across the river of time." The seer/soul traveler Paul Twitchell, ECKANKAR, and his analogy of an astral deck of cards to the Akashic Records was briefly covered. Tim went on to mention being introduced to psychic/artist Benn Lewis by Harold Salkin on a trip to Washington, DC (most likely the same trip mentioned below, while doing research for the Beckley/Salkin Saga article). Benn Lewis was involved with Soulcraft, "an international organization which has for its basis the second coming of Christ." Lewis not only believed in reincarnation, he claimed "22 confirmations that he is John the Apostle." Lewis, as an artist, would also channel "masters in the spirit world," and had paintings hung in both the White House and the Pentagon. Lewis, and the Soulcraft organization, believed in the prophecies from the Book of Revelations, in other words, world tribulation, the rule of an anti-Christ, and the mark on people's foreheads. Through meditation, the general message Lewis had received was one of "love, peace and concern for the present state of mankind." Tim compares this with messages others had received from alien intelligences that had been compiled in his *Book of Space Brothers*.

The next section of the column was titled, "Age of the Robots is Here," which describes Tim and Harold Salkin meeting Arnold Lestri and learning of an "Existential Computer," which sounds like something pulled from today's headlines, and the talk of artificial intelligence. Lestri worked for Andromeda, Inc., a computer company working on creating the Existential Computer, which Lestri claimed in ten years or less would be "the ultimate achievement in man's quest to duplicate the total functioning of the human brain." The super, super computer would be able to create artwork, write books, compose music, and all would be original. As well, it would "have consciousness, free will and emotional reaction." Its wonders continued, it would be "capable of 'suffering', of feeling pleasure, pain and anxiety," it could engage in reasoning, and to top it all off, "it will be able to reproduce itself."

The last section of the column was called "Astrology and Murder" in which Tim interviewed Barbara H. Watters, a leading Washington area astrologer and author of the book, *The Astrologer Looks At Murder* (1969). She believed "you can actually determine the real motives at work in criminal cases through the application of astrological forces." She had studied several high profile murder cases of which she found the infamous Lizzie Borden case of 1892 the most interesting; Watters had lived in Borden's home town of Fall River, Massachusetts for twenty years. Lizzie Borden was never convicted

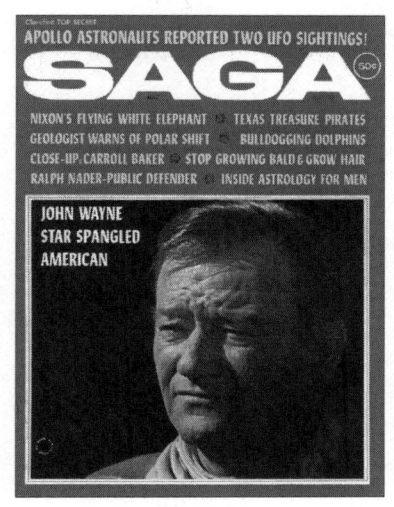

Saga May 1970

of the murder of her parents for lack of evidence. Watters had done an astrological chart for Lizzie and had determined that she was guilty. Watters also came up with a motive—Lizzie had wanted to improve her station in life. As Watters stated, "She was born with four planets in the sign of Leo. Statisically, Leo is under-represented in the charts of murderers. But it is a proud sign which does not bear frustration with good grace." In her previously mentioned book, Watters also revealed the identity of Jack the Ripper.

Saga magazine, was a long running men's adventure title that had started publishing articles on UFOs in the mid-sixties. The journalist Harold Salkin became sort of a journalistic mentor to Tim and they co-authored the article, "Apollo 12: Mysterious Encounters With Flying Saucers," which was published in *Saga*'s May 1970 (volume 40, #2) issue; which, I must point out, is the same month and year as the above mentioned *Search Magazine*. Nineteen

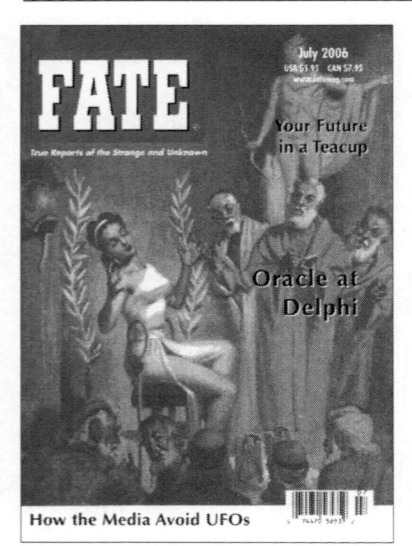

Fate July 2006

seventy seems to have been a pivotal year in Tim's writing career, as he says of the *Saga* article, "I do believe it's probably one of the most important in my career as a paranormal and UFO writer." Tim had gone to Washington, DC to do research for the article. Throughout the 1970s, Tim was regularly writing articles for *Saga UFO Report* and for their "UFO Specials." Tim also did an interview with Charles Berlitz, "Mr. Bermuda Triangle," in *Saga's Bermuda Triangle Special Report 1977*.

In the early 1970s, Tim was dealing with as many as thirty editors and magazine publishers looking for writing gigs and worked for many. This is how he met Art Crockett (1918–1990) and Bud Ampolsk (1922–2010), most likely at Reese Publishing, where the two were editing and writing for the magazine *Frontier West* and other Reese/Em-Tee true crime detective and men's adventure titles. Crockett and Ampolsk had written for the detective fiction pulp digests in the late fifties and early sixties such as *Manhunt*, *Off Beat Detective Stories*, *Sure Fire Detective Stories*, *Two-Fisted Detective Stories*, *Web Detective Stories*, *Mike Shayne Mystery Magazine*, *Shock Mystery Tales*, and so on.

Many of the UFO articles in the weekly national tabloids, from the late 1960s on, were written by Tim, usually anonymously, as he has been a stringer for the *National Enquirer*, *National Informer*, *National Tattler*, *Midnight Globe*, *National Star*, and others. Tim was also writing the adult film reviews for the early issues of *Hustler* in late 1975–76. He was the Editor-In-Chief for *Adult Cinema Review* in the early '80s for a spell, as well as writing for *Oui*, *Genesis*, *High Society*, and other men's sophisticate titles.

In 1977, Tim was a stringer for *Violent World* magazine; he packaged three issues of his *Front Page Disasters* magazine for Cousins Publishing; started his own tabloid, *UFO Review*, which lasted for over a decade; and was writing occasionally for Myron Fass at Countrywide Publishing where he met Jeff Goodman during Goodman's first week there. Tim wrote three articles for Countrywide's short lived *ESP* magazine and did some writing for some of Countrywide's rock magazines. And, in 1978 he edited three issues of the magazine *Future Fantasy* which were also published by Cousins Publishing.

With his paranormal publishing imprints, Inner Light/Global Communications and Conspiracy Journal Productions, Tim has published countless titles of his own as well as books by Art Crockett, Brad Steiger, Commander X, Tim Swartz, Sean

Casteel, and other noted authors of the paranormal. In 1980, the year of John Lennon's tragic assassination, Sunshine Publications, Inc. published the tribute paperbacks *Lennon: What Happened*, edited by Tim with Bud Ampolsk as one of the reporters, and *Lennon: Up Close & Personal*, edited by Tim with Art Crockett as one of the writers. That same year, Tim and Jeff Goodman themselves published a thin tabloid of photos of John Lennon taken in New York City titled, *Lennon As We Knew Him*. And, Tim edited the two magazines, *UFO Universe* (1988–98) and *Unsolved UFO Sightings*, which were published by GCR. More recently, he has written articles for *UFO Magazine* whose publisher was William J. Birnes.

Tim had a cover article in *Fate*'s July 2006 issue (volume 59, #7, issue 675) titled, "On the Trail of the Oracle of Delphi: A Seasoned Journeyman Explores the Secrets of An Ancient Mystery by Timothy Green Beckley as told to Sean Casteel." The issue also contained articles by two long-time friends of Tim's, "Reporting On UFOs" by Tim R. Swartz, and "Haunted Writer's Retreat" by Brad Steiger. The cover painting had been originally used on *Fate*'s July 1955 issue which had the article, "Secrets of the Delphi Oracle." Pilgrimages to the Temple on Mount Parnassus had been part of its thousand-year-long history as the omphalos of the ancient world, starting in the 8th century B.C. In Tim's article, he tells of his journey to Greece with his friend, seeress Penny Melis, who was of Greek heritage, and their experiences, both intellectual and psychic, to the center of an ancient mystery religion at the Temple of Apollo at Delphi.

Tim wrote, "We were 100 miles from the traffic-snarled, smog-drenched capitol of Athens, and had soon come to realize that those who live in the Greek highlands to the northeast are more accustomed to the simpler life, as they have lived for thousands of years." Penny regaled Tim with the myths and legends of the of the Temple of Apollo and its Oracle, as Tim did some video-taping on their arduous mile-long climb up to the site. They were on a "vision quest." And, ultimately, Penny did have a vision of an oracle, an older woman with "cloudy eyes" of whom she inquired, "I wanted to know where my life is going, and what I should do?" The answer she received was, "You can make yourself happy through your next steps." Penny then asked, "So what steps do I take?" And, the Oracle answered back, "You have to make your own path and find your own happiness." Penny determined she had "lost her way" in life and, had strayed from the path she had been on, that of a "devoted witch," she had sunk into more materialistic concerns, and had to get back on her path of happiness. Tim concluded, ". . . when Penny and I touched the fabric of time . . . it reached out and touched us back."

The legendary oracular powers have historically been ascribed to mysterious sweet smelling vapors that seeped up through the floor of the temple over which the Oracle would sit on a tripod-legged chair. These were thought to be rising up from a fault-line crack under the temple which would put the Oracle in prophetic mode. At first, that theory was disproved by the original

Timothy Green Beckley and Tom Brinkmann at the Museum of Sex in New York City in 2005. Photo by Jeff Goodman.

excavation of the site in the early twentieth-century proving it did not sit on a fault-line from which the vapors were thought to come. But, more recently Delphi was found to be built on the crux of two fault-lines and it was determined scientifically that the gas ethylene was the cause of the Oracle's ecstatically ambiguous prophecies, giving answers that could be interpreted in more than one way; hence, the famous maxims inscribed over the entrance to the temple, "Know Thy Self," and "Everything In Moderation."

In summary, Timothy Green Beckley, "Mr. UFO," the man in blue, is a noted ufologist, researcher, writer, editor, publisher, rock 'n' roller, radio personality, videographer, and podcaster. In other words, a man that is prolific and has worn many hats in his five-decade career. In 2013, Tim had a pacemaker put in and says, "Health problems are still an issue—am half dead; but the half that is alive is really rocking."

Look for Tim's "Mr. UFO's Secret UFO Files" on YouTube and, "Exploring the Bizarre With Timothy Beckley and Tim R. Swartz" on the KCOR Digital Radio Network every Thursday night—also on YouTube.

References & Suggested Reading

Beckley, Timothy Green. *Shirley MacLaine Meets The Pleiadians*. New Brunswick, NJ: Global Communications/Conspiracy Journal, 2015.

Beckley, Timothy Green. *Strange Encounters*. New Brunswick, NJ: Inner Light, 1992, 2007.

Beckley, Timothy Green. *Timothy Green Beckley's Strange Saga: Updated Edition*. New Brunswick, NJ: Global Communications/Conspiracy Journal, 2013.

Nadis, Fred. *The Man From Mars: Ray Palmer's Amazing Pulp Journey*. New York, NY: Jeremy P. Tarcher/Penguin, 2013.

Bad Mags volume one and two
by Tom Brinkmann

Available from amazon.com

Manhunt Dec. 1953
Review by Richard Krauss

Manhunt: the gold standard of hardboiled crime fiction digests. One look at the line-up for this issue tells you why. David Goodis opens with "Black Pudding," the dark, sweet, just dessert of revenge. That's Ken and Tillie on the cover, painted by Frank Uppwall. Pretty girl, but then you're looking at her good side. Ken's first impression: "It was a female voice, sort of a cracked whisper. It had a touch of asthma in it, some alcohol, and something else that had no connection with health or happiness." He's fresh out of San Quentin, with plans for a fresh start in Philly that turn dire when his past suddenly flashes a five-inch blade in the dark.

The premise of Richard Marsten's "Switch Ending" is remarkably similar to "Black Pudding." How long does it take an ex-con's old cronies to make trouble once he's back on the streets? It this case, Danny joins the trouble in progress and attempts to set things right. But he's living in a dark, noir world, and the best he can manage is to trade one evil for another.

"Killing on Seventh Street" by Charles Beckman, Jr. is a psychological thriller. A regular Joe kills a robber/rapist and struggles with how the violent act has changed him. "But, that evening, he was behind the garage, sharpening the lawn mower, when the neighborhood dog came running over, barking. Clifford reached for the animal and things dissolved in a haze. When it cleared, the dog was a limp form, its broken neck clenched in this hands."

"Murder Marches On" by Craig Rice features series character John J. Malone. In this adventure the slight lawyer must simply liaise a list of names from a witness to the authorities, as said witness prefers to remain anonymous. Perhaps for the sake of its drama, the exchange takes place in a parade with Malone dressed for the part. At the designated moment chaos erupts and the list holder is murdered. Malone is left with five pages to ensure he's not the next victim, solve the murder, find the list and collect his fee from his now deceased client. Fortunately, he's in good hands with Rice.

Things turn considerably darker in "Sucker" by Hunt Collins. Arrested for the rape and murder of his babysitter, Harley appeals to his

Manhunt Vol. 1 #12 December 1953, cover by Frank Uppwall.

friend and lawyer, Dave, to help clear him. At the trial the prosecutor's case, built on a chain of circumstantial evidence, is riddled with doubts by the time Dave finishes. Trouble is, so is Dave.

"Portrait of a Killer" was a regular true crime feature written for *Manhunt* most often by Dan Sontup. The series began in August 1953 and ran twenty-four issues, ending in July 1955. This issue devotes three pages to Portrait #7, Tillie Gburek, a serial killer who started out poisoning neighborhood dogs and then moved up to a succession of husbands.

The "The Wife of Riley" by Evan

Hunter, concerns the disappearance of Riley's wife at a seashore resort. The place is run by an untoward dude, rife with hidden agendas. "His skin was bad and his eyes were puffed with sleep, and he looked like the kind of guy you could rouse out of any doorway in the Bowery." Tension mounts as Riley strips away the resort's façade of normalcy to learn the where and why of his wife's sudden vanishing act.

Scott Jordan was a series character created by Harold Q. Masur. The lawyer/sleuth takes on a new client in the "Richest Man in the Morgue." It's one of several Jordan stories for *Manhunt*, later collected in *The Name is Jordan* (1962). "Morgue" is a top-notch yarn with some terrific writing. Here's one of Masur's punchy asides: "They thought Hitler was nothing but a windbag too, until he gave the world twenty-four hours to get out."

Some of *Manhunt*'s stories are so dark, they could easily have run in a horror magazine. For example, "The Quiet Room" by Jonathan Craig features a dirty cop and his dirty partner. She beats up underage prostitutes in the soundproof room at the precinct to learn the names of the girl's johns. Then he blackmails the johns to keep their criminal activity off the record. Things end badly.

"The Coyote" by David Chandler features a father who forces his son to "be a man" by killing a coyote. It's brutal and torturous, and unfortunately, an accurate portrayal of doctrine over common sense.

Roy Carroll's characters face personal and social atrocity in "Wife Beater." Officer Tom Rivas grew up in a house where dad beat mom. Perhaps Cherry Szykora did

too. Both wrestle with their pasts as they try to rectify their present.

"The Icepick Artists" by Frank Kane is listed on the contents page as a novelette. It is, but it's also the first part of a longer saga that involves the death of a PI employed by Seaway Indemnity. The firm hires Johnny Liddell to investigate. He solves the murder, but the larger criminal mastermind waits for readers and Liddell in a follow-up adventure in the January 1954 edition.

"Crime Cavalcade" presents a rapid-fire succession of short true crime stories in newspaper style. The feature ran from May 1953 through December 1955, handled by Vincent H. Gaddis. Here's a example: "As a gag to illustrate low salaries, Bruce Shanks, cartoonist for the *Evening News* in Buffalo, N.Y., pictured a policeman baby-sitting to supplement his regular salary. However some of the paper's readers didn't get the point. Half a dozen parents telephoned police headquarters that night seeking baby sitters."

The issue's final yarn, "The Insecure" by R. Van Taylor was billed as "... one of the most unusual ideas ever to appear in *Manhunt*." It's more like something out of the *Twilight Zone* than a traditional crime anthology, but once you're tuned in to its unreliable narrator, its an entertaining twist on the expected.

If this edition is any indication, it's small wonder *Manhunt* remains the premier title for fans and collectors of hard-boiled crime fiction digests.

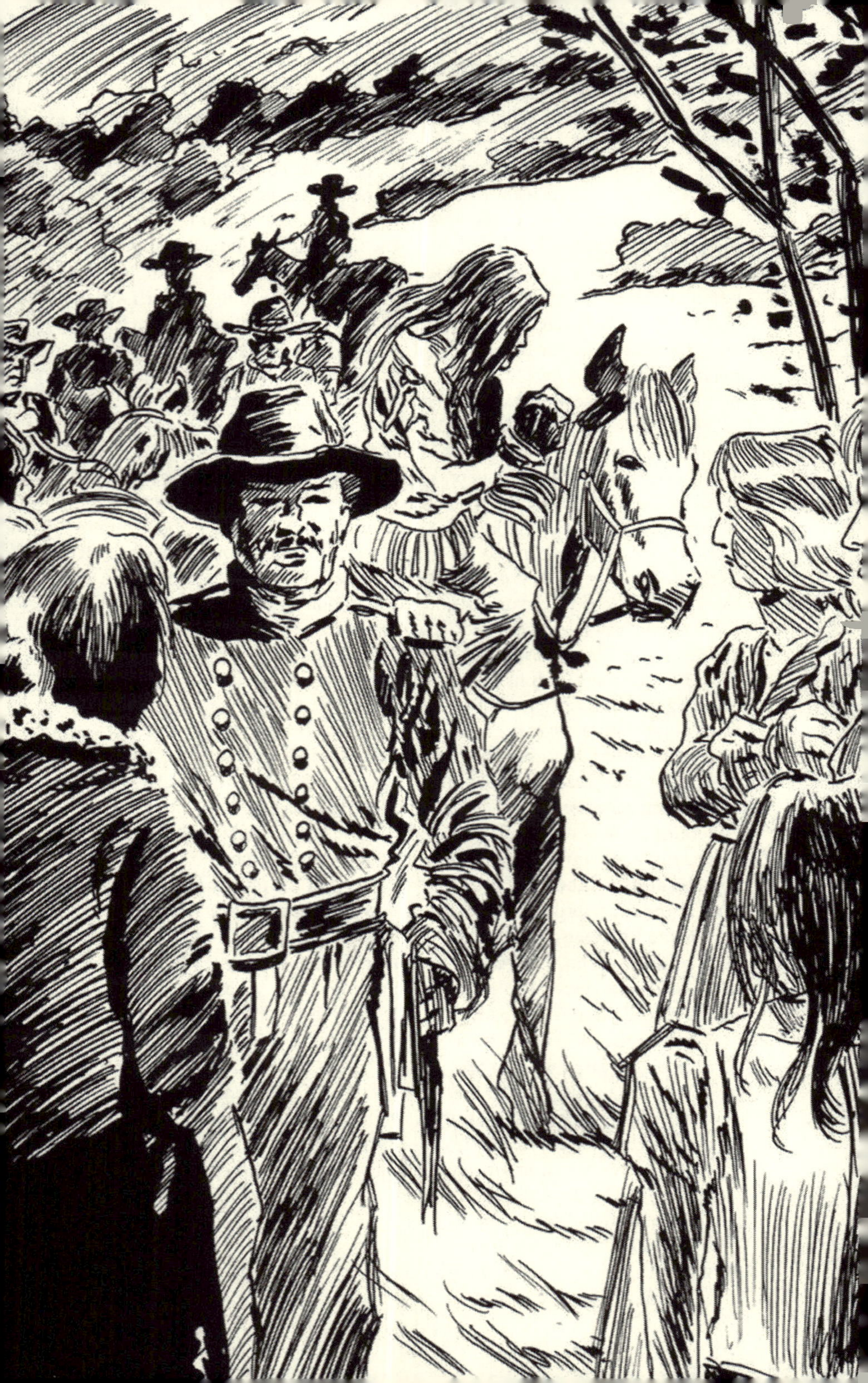

Old Aunt Sin

Western fiction by Gary Lovisi
Illustrations by Michael Neno

"Appears to me, mam, that woman's got a long way to go to get civilized. She's got a lot of fight in her and she'll have to be broken first, like a spring colt, and forced to obey."

I'd heard the stories about her from my ma and all the other daughters of General Abrams over the years. Old Aunt Sin, Aunt Cynthia Abrams, tough, crotchety, often nasty. They say she cussed like a Virginia City silver miner, could shoot better than Captain Adam H. Bogardus himself, and had kilt more Indians than Buffalo Bill or Kit Carson when she'd been in her prime. She was an old-timer now but there was still talk she'd been a beau of Sam Houston back in '42 after Texas had won its independence from Mexico. They said Aunt Cynthia had even turned him down. In fact, she'd never married. It was all because of what the Indians did. She hated Indians and so did I. But I think I was even more scared of Aunt Sin than any Indians back then in 1876. I was just twelve years old, but I remember Ma threatening us with her when we was youngins. "Behave, or we'd be sent packing to live with Old Aunt Sin!" That got results, let me tell ya.

Aunt Sin's ma and the General had first come out here in '35 with their first two daughters, the oldest being Cynthia and the youngest three-year-old Mary. That was more than 40 years ago. Not long before little Mary had been taken away by Comanches and never seen again. Aunt Sin never stopped talking about what had happened that terrible day the Indians swooped upon their wagon. She never forgot her little sister. She told my ma and all her younger sisters about the wild savage red men who ruled the plains and put terror into everyone on the prairie ever since she could remember. We never forgot Mary. Aunt Sin made sure of that. So I guess it was right natural that we figured the only good Indian was a dead Indian, as Aunt Sin often said, but she wasn't the only one who felt that way. I was powerful scared of the red devils myself, even though I'd never seen any of the real wild ones—just 'tame' ones sometimes in town who seemed just like anyone else to me. They seemed real sad to look at, kinda wore out, tired. Those Indians sure didn't scare me. But I was an almost growed up girl of twelve by then and so I was growing out of my Indian fear. Least I thought so.

That was until the Army said they'd tracked down a band of renegades. They went right down into the Mexican hills to get them—trapped them all and found out that among their squaws they had discovered a white woman! It turned out to be my lost Aunt Mary!

My ma told me the soldiers were bringing her back to us. "She's family, Kathleen, and she's white like us—though God alone knows what those red devils did to her all these years. At least she'll be back with her own kind now. Finally. Been over 40 years. My, my!"

At twelve I couldn't conceive of being 40 years away from home and hearth and what that might be like. I tried to conjure it up and it came to over three of my own lifetimes!

"What's she like, Ma?" I asked, full of curious questions.

"Don't rightly know, chile, she's been gone long. Likely she's turned squaw on us, but she's still your Aunt Mary and she's a'coming home at last. I know the family and all her sisters will be pleased to have her back after so long. Especially Aunt Sin."

I kinda doubted that.

All five of the General's daughters, my ma and my four aunts, were soon abuzz over the fact that lost little Aunt Mary was coming home to us after so long. The Army captain, name of Wilson, said a detachment of his troopers were bringing her in and that they'd have her at our house any day now.

Ma, being the only one of the five sisters married and with a home of her own that was in a central location, was naturally chosen as the place where they'd bring Aunt Mary. Ma's sisters, all of whom lived nearby were there waiting. Except Old Aunt Sin, who lived way up in Tulsa. She had yet to arrive. Aunt Sin being the oldest daughter was the family matriarch, and the only one alive who had actually seen little Mary—over 40 years ago—and the only one who had not arrived yet to see the wild Indian woman come back to white civilization where she belonged.

'Wild' wasn't the word for what I heard Captain Wilson tell my ma and pa about Aunt Mary. She barked at night, smelled like a ripe buffalo, and did a number of Indian things that no white woman would ever think of doing. She also tried to escape.

"She's a fighter, that one. Not a speck of white left in her. Them damn red devils made a squaw out of her. She's been breeding young bucks for christsakes, more for us to hunt down and kill I suspect," the captain said.

"She's still family," my ma said, "and once we get her here, me and my sisters will civilize her, Captain."

"Appears to me, mam, that woman's got a long way to go to get civilized. She's got a lot of fight in her and she'll have to be broken first, like a spring colt, and forced to obey."

"I'm sure she'll be fine once we get her here and into proper clothes and all, Captain."

"Well, my men are gonna break her of some of her foolish habits so she won't run away from you and go back to them thieving redskins."

"Thank you, Captain."

Captain Wilson nodded, tipped his hat, "Least we can do, mam."

Little lost Mary turned out to be a 50-year-old Indian squaw woman who looked older than Grandma did when she died at 70. The Army troopers had her hands and legs tied and a gag was shoved in her mouth. She was in torn rags and dirty and she smelled bad.

My ma ordered the troopers, "Untie her right now! And get that gag out of her mouth!"

Captain Wilson nodded to his men to do as she told them.

My ma then went over to Aunt Mary, who was dressed in fringed buckskin and cotton leggings, moccasins, like a squaw. She sat silent upon the Army horse, head down. We could hardly see her face, it was covered with long black hair streaked with gray. My ma smiled up at her and said, "Mary! It's so good to finally see you! Welcome home, sister!"

Ma beckoned for Mary to get down from the horse. I don't think Aunt Mary could speak American any more after so many years. She'd only been five when she'd been stolen away. She didn't look like she knew what was happening to her. She tried to make sounds, then spoke rapidly in Indian talk.

"That's Comanche, mam," Captain Wilson said. "She don't speak no English no more."

"That's all right, Captain," my mom said. "We'll have her right as rain once we give her a bath and get her out of those terrible smelly Indian cloths and into a nice gingham dress."

I saw the Captain nod without much conviction. Then he told his men to mount up and they rode off leaving Aunt Mary with me, my mom, and her three sisters, all of us not knowing what to do and waiting for Old Aunt Sin to arrive and tell us what to do.

It was supposed to be the happiest day in Aunt Mary's life. She was back with her kith and kin. Back with her sisters. Saved from the red devils. Back with civilized white people once more and away from her prison of savagery. Or so Ma and her sisters said over and over again. I knew they was disappointed though. Aunt Mary was supposed to be one of them but she didn't act like them. In fact, she didn't really seem happy to be "saved" at all.

"I'm 'fraid Little Mary's been squawed plum out of her mind," my Aunt Kate said one evening when all the sisters was meeting together, except Old Aunt Sin of course, who we was still waiting upon.

"Damn Indians made her one of them now, but we'll get Little Mary back! We'll teach her!" That was Aunt Jane, a proper, spare the rod and spoil the child teacher over in Elk Grove. She always said how her favorite medicine was a long, limber switch put to purposeful use upon the back of a youngin. I cringed, for I knew she was itching to put that switch to use on the Indian parts of Aunt Mary. I began to feel sad for Aunt Mary, seeing as how she was woven together with both red Indian parts, and the white Abrams parts that was my blood and kin.

Aunt Mary for her own part was unresponsive to it all. She just sat in her room. On the floor. Not eating. Not drinking. Staring at the blank wall like it wasn't there, almost as though she could see right through it. I wondered what she could be looking at. It was the strangest thing. There was a large window on the other side of the room that she could have easily looked out of, but she ignored that. She just sat there, staring at that blank wall, like she was watching some Indian spirits or such. Sometimes she'd make little sounds, secret Indian talk,

I figured. I watched her from the hallway, afraid to enter her room, afraid to leave and miss out on her odd doings. Wondering all the time what was going on in her head.

I figured she'd try to escape out her opened second floor window first chance she got. She didn't even try. When I asked my ma about it, she told me, "No, honey, Aunt Mary won't be doing no escaping from this house."

I said I didn't understand.

It was prim Aunt Jane who told me, "Those nice trooper boys did us a favor and took all the fight out of her troublesome squaw nature, that's why."

I found out later "taking the fight out of her," meant to tie her hand and foot and dump her over a saddle for traveling. Have her gagged for

days and unfed so she wouldn't be strong or spry. Unable to give no trouble. In the beginning I heard they "softened her up" by running her with a rope bound to her wrists from behind a horse. When she fell, the horse dragged her. I found out later that's why she had been so dirty and smelled so bad when I'd first seen her brought in.

I began to wish Aunt Mary would escape but she just sat there, softly crying Indian songs. Escaping in her mind, maybe, but her body was definitely not going anywhere.

My ma wasn't always around. She had a caring heart, even if Mary was all Indian now. My Aunt Kate and Aunt Jane were different. They hated Indians and they showed it. I think they hated Mary too. They forced Mary to bathe, which I figured was a good thing. They also forced her to strip and wear new clean white woman's clothes, which I also thought was a good thing. But it's the way they did it that bothered me. They were hurtful. Harsh. And they seemed to enjoy it. I told Ma one time that I saw Aunt Jane switching Aunt Mary, but she told me I had to be mistaken and paid me no mind. I know I wasn't mistaken.

Next day I saw the welts on Mary's back and I cried as I hugged her to me. She sang Indian songs low, almost silent. They were sad songs. I saw tears and that faraway look in her eyes. I wanted to help her escape and told her so, but she could not understand me, nor respond in any way.

Aunt Jane said, "I swear, our squaw sister is the most persistent Indian. But don't fear, once Old Aunt Sin gets here, she'll put the fire of resoluteness in Mary and cure her of all her evil Indian ways."

That's what I was afraid of.

The Overland Stage came in town the next day. A buckboard was sent out by Pa to bring Old Aunt Sin, Aunt Cynthia Abrams, to our ranch outside of town.

We all waited. Curious. Once we saw the buckboard approach with riders, Army Captain Wilson and some men alongside, everyone came outside to watch. Aunt Kate and Aunt Jane went to fetch Aunt Mary. They had to force, carry and prod her into the hot outside sun. And there we all stood watching the long flat plain ahead as the buckboard and calvery riders churned up dust on the long winding dirt road as they slowly approached our house.

Ma said, "It's Aunt Sin, alright. I can see her hair from here. Still blazing like an avenging angel of the Lord, bless her."

"She'll cure our little Indian," Aunt Jane said giving a harsh look over to Aunt Mary, who was sitting silently in the dirt, her face down, her mind a million miles away.

I went over to her and put my arm around her, hugging her, whispering, "Don't worry, Aunt Mary, I'll protect you." She never looked at me, never spoke, all I felt was a wave of deep sadness from her. She was so alone, so helpless. And now Aunt Sin was getting closer and closer and I was scared now of what that would mean.

Once the buckboard had approached and stopped, and the soldiers and Captain Wilson dismounted, I saw Old Aunt Sin up close. She was covered in black clothing and a cape, all dusty from her travels, and a dark scarf that covered her face from the road dust. Only her bright red hair stood up above the scarf. It was fire-red bright. She looked like fire herself.

Slowly she eased herself out of the buckboard, Captain Wilson offered his hand, as any gentleman would to a lady, but Old Aunt Sin true to her type slapped it away.

"I ain't dead yet, dammit! I think I can still motivate this old behind up and around without any help."

Captain Wilson backed off.

I saw Ma smile.

Pa just shook his head. He wanted no part of this. To him it was "between the sisters" as he'd told me. He walked off to do some chores.

Aunt Jane hit her switch against her palm impatiently, saying, "Finally! Now we'll get to the bottom of this foolishness and get Mary acting white again!"

I just held my Aunt Mary tighter and realized something I never felt before. I hated my Aunt Jane and I was scared to death of Aunt Sin.

Aunt Sin greeted my ma and her other sisters gruffly, no fancy talk or hugs, just plain, "Alright now, let's get to the real reason I'm here and traveled all this damn way. God knows it wasn't to see any of you again! Sisters? Huh! Where is my Mary?"

"Mary?" Ma asked, then pointed, "She's over there with my daughter, Kathleen, Cynthia."

Aunt Sin leveled her gaze at me with cold and small eyes that looked like snake eyes. Her red fire-hair flamed in front of me. She unwrapped her scarf and for the first time I could see her entire face. She must have been very beautiful when she'd been young. Her skin was so fair and clean, so bright and ... radiant was the only word I could think of. Like a star. She shone. Even at her advanced age. She had a stern mouth, an overall visage that was hard. You knew she had seen a hard life and given hardness in return, you also knew she brooked no foolishness. Her eyes told you that she could back up her words and that you should never make the mistake of pressing her too hard.

I gulped and held Aunt Mary tighter.

"Who ... are ... you?" she growled looking down at me.

My ma came over then, "Why, Cynthia, you remember me writing you about my daughter, Kathleen?"

"Hah! She's growed quite a bit, almost a woman now, I expect!"

"I'm near thirteen years old, Aunt Sin," I said.

She stared at me. Hard. I didn't know what she was looking at. Maybe me sitting there in the dirt with my arms around her sister Mary? I didn't know really what, or why.

Finally she shook her head in frustration, "Youngins!"

I smiled.

She did not return my smile.

I got nervous then. Fearful. For myself and for Aunt Mary. Old Aunt Sin was scary.

"And Mary?" she asked firmly.

My ma pointed to the limp figure sitting in the dirt so silently beside me.

Then Old Aunt Sin did something I never expected at all. She came over and sat down in the dirt right in front of us. Right there in the dirt with her fine cloths and all like it didn't matter one bit to her. It was shocking, but no one there had the will to mutter a word. Then she whispered, "Mary?"

Aunt Mary did not respond at all.

Old Aunt Sin

Aunt Sin quietly repeated, "Mary?" Then she reached out and gently lifted up her sister's chin so they could look into each other's eyes.

For a long moment the two women looked at each other. Neither one saying a word. From where I was I saw a tear drop from each of the woman's eyes.

Old Aunt Sin so stern and hard, her gaze boring into Aunt Mary's eyes. Questioning. Curious.

Aunt Mary silent, so sad. Yet they seemed to be communicating—though not one word was spoken.

Aunt Jane finally broke the spell saying, "Cynthia, you should use this on her," offering the switch to her older sister. I could see that it was dark with spots, not green like it had been days past. I knew that switch had tasted blood and I did not want to think about it.

"You used that on her?" Aunt Cynthia asked quietly.

"Once or twice so far," Aunt Jane responded with a shrug. "It is the only way we can get any reaction out of her. I tell you if Mary won't leave those Indian ways of hers we'll have to beat them out of her."

Old Aunt Sin just nodded grimly. I froze up inside. I felt all was lost then for my Aunt Mary. I waited, knowing something more was coming from Aunt Sin.

Then Old Aunt Sin screwed up her face into a cranky grimace and added, "Why Jane, appears to me you and all the family been making the damnedest mistake thinking that this here Indian woman be our long lost kin, Mary.

It ain't so at all, I tell you."

My eyes darted up to Old Aunt Sin in surprise. Aunt Jane, my ma, the other sisters, all looked to Aunt Sin in confusion and for some sort of explanation.

"Why, whatever do you mean, Cynthia?" Aunt Jane asked, totally flummoxed.

"Ain't it plain to you? Well, it's as plain to me as the nose on your face, Jane. I'm the only one remembers my beloved sister Mary, and I tell you now, that this here Indian woman ain't her."

There was alarm and consternation now. I couldn't believe how mean Aunt Sin could be denying her own sister—for I had no doubt that she was Aunt Mary—but what she said next made me angry with her too.

"And another thing," Aunt Sin growled now as if angry herself, "I don't cotton to the idea of us taking red devil squaws into our family. I think it best that you make sure this Indian is delivered back to her people where she belongs right away. Get her out of here! But treat her respectful, give her a horse and food, then send her on her way home. And now, I'm going back home to Tulsa. Damn bunch of fools calling me all the way out here for nothing! And at my advanced age, too! Why, I could catch my death!"

Then Old Aunt Sin turned around, her back now to her sisters and the rest of the family. When no one could see, she looked straight in my eyes and I froze meeting her gaze, but she only smiled at me and winked, saying, "Come here, young Kathleen. Help your Old Aunt Cynthia into the buckboard. That's a good girl. I'm going home now." And then she whispered to me, "And so is our little Mary. Back to the only home she's known these 40 long years."

I rode the buckboard with Old Aunt Sin into town where she'd catch the Overland Stage back to Tulsa. On the way out we saw Aunt Mary riding bareback on one of our sleek little mares. She rode like the wind, back to the only home she'd ever known. Back to the only family she ever really had. She was free now. She whooped and hollered when she passed us by, and Old Aunt Sin stood up on the buckboard and whooped and hollered back at her.

That's when I knew the real Aunt Sin.

That's when we became fast friends as well as just kin.

↙ ↙

Gary Lovisi is an author, also a bookseller and collector who writes about collectable paperbacks. Under his Gryphon Books imprint, he publishes *Paperback Parade*, the world's leading magazine on collectable paperbacks of all kinds. You can find out more about him and his work at his website: gryphonbooks.com

---

The Digest Enthusiast book one
- Interview with *Fate* editor Phyllis Galde
- Interview with *Fantasy & Science Fiction* editor Gordon Van Gelder
- Archie Digest Library
- *Galaxy Science Fiction*
- Digests of Myron Fass
- Walter Gibson's *The Big Story*
- Reviews
- Fiction
- And much more

Available from amazon.com
$8.99 print, $2.99 Kindle

Children's Digest Spring 1972
Review by Richard Krauss

Children's Digest relied heavily on re-presenting material from earlier sources. Considering its audience, some of its dated sentiments are even more alarming than those in magazines of its era intended for adults. For example, in the lead story, "The Railway Children" by E. Nesbit, a young girl faints as she and two other children attempt to flag down a train headed for an unseen, deadly wreck. After she recovers, her sibling's reaction: "And presently, when she stopped crying, they were able to laugh at her for being such a coward as to faint."

I purchased this particular issue as a sample due to Jerry Robinson's cover feature "From Cave Drawing to Comic Strip" which presents a brief history of the form. It's a competent overview and includes a good assortment of comic strip character illustrations, but clearly simplified for its intended audience.

The issue's best feature is part four of "King Ottokar's Sceptre," from "The Adventures of Tintin," which ran in *CD* from 1966 thru 1979. Perhaps other issues gave readers more, but this one reprints only two pages of comics in black-and-white. Maybe it's because they're accompanied by eight pages of "history" about the fictitious country of Syldavia, with some beautiful supporting artwork by Hergé.

In all, the issue reprints six short stories that run from four to seventeen pages in length. All include good quality illustrations, some in a more detailed classic illustration style and some with a modern 1970s look. Nearly all take advantage of the magazine's two color printing.

In addition to Robinson's article on comic strips, three other articles appear: "Was There Ever Such a Bird as a Dodo?," "Water Snails" and "Take Off With Books." The latter being two pages of reviews of children's books.

I imagine the balance, the "fun and activities" pages, were favorites among subscribers. They feature an assortment of puzzles, jokes, a pancake recipe (inspired by Winnie-the-Pooh), and puzzle solutions.

Children's Digest was "famously" printed on "eye ease" ever-so-slightly tinted paper. "This light green paper is easier on the eyes than white or any other tinted paper."

↙

Fate #727
Review by Richard Krauss

With its best cover in recent memory and its headline story: Marie Laveau, Voodoo High Priestess, *Fate* #727 provides a powerful first impression. In "I See by the Papers," the *Fate* Staff provides the inside story on the cover painting. It's a 1977 oil on wood by Charles Massicot Gandolfo, who founded the Voodoo Museum in 1972 and had to rely on first-hand impressions to create his portrait of Laveau (1801–1881) as no known photographs or verified portraits exist. The balance of "…the Papers" is culled from *The Week*, *Reader's Digest*, an NBC affiliate WFLA, the Associated Press and the *San Francisco Chronicle*.

"From Your Editor" by Phyllis Galde begins with a bombshell. While meditating, Galde attempted to contact Marie Laveau and heard the sounds of her "rich, full, and deep" voice! Other events in Galde's life include the adoption of a new puppy and DNA testing through 23andme.

I have to admit after the cover image and the initial bits about Marie Laveau in the opening columns, my anticipation was primed for the cover story. Brad Steiger's report begins with a Voodoo Head Washing Ceremony conducted by Mambo Sallie Anne Glassman, one of the most active Voodoo practitioners in the United States today. It's there, at the New Orleans Healing Center, that a new shrine created by Ricardo Pustanio, was installed to pay tribute to the reigning Voodoo priestess of the nineteenth century, Marie Laveau. Laveau succeeded Mama Sanite Dede in about 1830, as High Priestess. The article touches on several fascinating events in the Voodoo Queen's life, but at just five pages, I can't help wishing there were far more.

The "Interview with Wade Davis" follows suit. It's one page, more like a recap of highlights than an actual interview loaded with quotations. It's a transitional piece that steers the topic of voodoo toward zombies, which is the subject of Micah Hanks' following article, "Feast of Flesh."

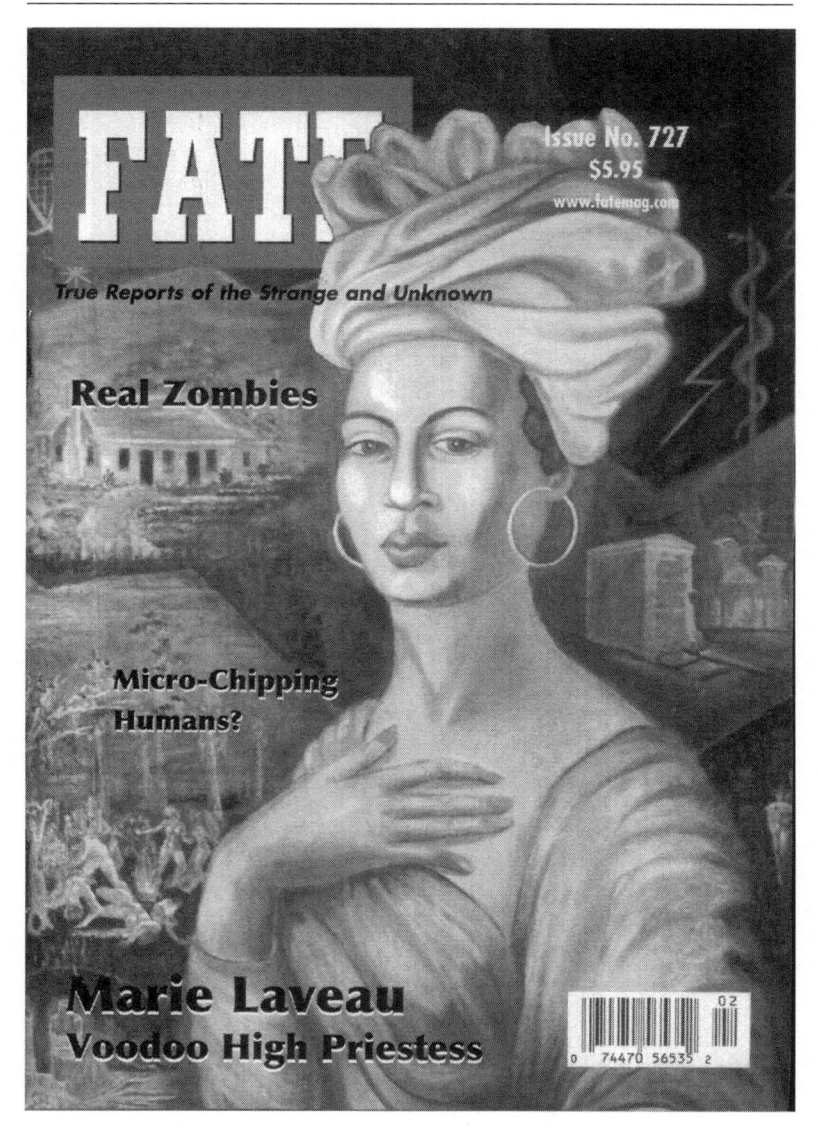

Hanks cites "mankind's long-held fascination with death, and reanimation" in movies and religion, and the rise of zombies in popular culture. Even FEMA and the CDC leverage an imaginary zombie apocalypse as a springboard for emergency preparedness. Thankfully after the introduction things get serious and the case of Clairvius Narcisse is examined through the research of the aforementioned Wade Davis. Davis wrote a whole book on the subject, *The Serpent and the Rainbow* 1985. "A Harvard scientist's astonishing journey into the secret societies of Haitian voodoo, zombis, and magic." Unlike fictional zombies that feed on human flesh, zombification by voodoo produces a near-death state and potential enslavement through mind control. Like most supernatural phenomena the evidence for zombies is inconclusive. You either want to believe or not.

"Lily Dale is the oldest community dedicated to the practice of the Spiritualist Religion," reports Ron Nagy in his exploration of the place and its fascinating history, which began in 1844. Today, "Activities include workshops for New Age ideas, healing techniques, basic Spiritualism classes, ghost walks, and sweat lodges." Search on "Lily Dale Assembly" for more information.

Wendy Barker, author of *A Stubborn Willful Girl*, proclaims in "Wake up! Your Reshimot is Calling," a ten-week class in the Science of Kabbalah, has given her life new meaning and invites *Fate*'s readers to learn more about it for themselves.

Deborah Painter reports on her visit to Flatwoods, West Virginia, "Home of the Green Monster." On September 12, 1952 several UFO sightings were reported in West Virginia and Maryland. The most significant being just outside Flatwoods, where a group of teenagers accompanied by one adult witnessed ". . . a flashing, reddish object, shaped like a teardrop…" and "A very frightening thing with a small head . . ." The next day local reporters returned to the scene but found only a flattened circle of "tar grass," the only evidence supporting the witnesses' recollections. Painter summarizes the events described by several witnesses and subsequent investigators and leaves it to readers to draw their own conclusions.

In "A Drowned Eden?" Valenya posits the location of the Garden of Eden, The Great Flood, and the origins of the gods (ETs?) in a far-ranging article peppered with snarky asides.

Carl Llewellyn Weschcke is a former publisher of *Fate* and Chairman of Llewellyn Worldwide, a publisher of books for body, mind and spirit. In this edition he presents the second installment of the "Case of Joy Ann Erickson Upham," a missing person since late 2013. A former writer for Llwelleyn Publications, Upham later married and relocated to Texas, where she had two children and worked as an obstetrics nurse. Enlisting the aid of a group of volunteer psychic researchers, Weschcke reports on the events felt to have led to her disappearance after stopping at a liquor store near her home, and her likely death shortly thereafter.

Nick Redfern presents a cautionary scenario in which microchips could be implanted and used to make the world of Big Brother a reality. It's an excerpt from his *Secret History Conspiracies from Ancient Aliens to the New World Order* from Visible Ink Press, 2015.

A psychic connection between two psychics, one here and one on the other side, uncovers an alleged treaty made between an alien race and the U.S. government during the Eisenhower administration, according to Patricia Griffin Ross in her report on the source of many recent "Missing Persons." *Fate*'s content often borders on the unbelievable, but this entry crosses over.

"Is There a Real World Hogworts?" is an enticing question Michael Peter Langevin uses to pique interest in his article about the Monroe Institute, where experiential education programs facilitate the personal exploration of human consciousness, based in Faber, Virginia.

Another organization, this one dedicated to future oriented research, is the Arlington Institute, headed by John L. Petersen. His forward to *Infinite Energy Technologies*, edited by Finley Eversole, PH.D. is represented here. It's about change. In fact, "... our present century will see one thousand times the technological change of the past century..." The implications are beyond imagination. The new world will "... operate in very different ways." Thought control? Unlimited energy? Control of gravity? Who can say? But the changes will be rapid and our civil and social systems will struggle to keep pace or collapse as new systems emerge. Petersen provides some fascinating observations, which make his piece one of the issue's most intriguing.

Olav Phillips recounts "An Encounter with the Unknown" and the mysterious lights over Dixon, California that occurred more than two decades ago. Today, Phillips remains convinced what he and his girlfriend witnessed over several hours qualify as UFOs. If we are actively searching the skies for "them" should it be a surprise that "they" are also looking for us?

As if to support the idea, the reprint "Earthman, Stay Home!" from the March 1963 *Fate* appears next. The "Gulliver" instrument package designed for a Mars landing is described by Paul Foght, who gives strong caution to what it might find there and potential repercussions. Reading it now is amusing, but at the time it may have been alarming.

A second reprint, from a month later appears as well. It's by Dutch parapsychologist Dr. H.J. Fisher, who cites select writings of Dr. Albert Schweitzer about unexplained events to counter the humanitarian's own assertions that all psychic phenomena is merely superstition.

Micah Hanks returns with the second part of his "Beyond the Unknown" series to challenge a statement attributed to Sir Stephen Hawking: "... philosophy is dead. Philosophers have not kept up with modern developments in science, particularly physics."

The back pages are letters from readers sharing details of their own inexplicable encounters; advertisements (many of which feature interesting offers and claims); "My Proof of Survival," readers' factual accounts of survival after death; "True Mystic Experiences," personal accounts of paranormal events; and book reviews by *Fate* staffers.

Now a tradition, the final page recounts the latest communications from the afterlife from the late David Godwin, through the medium Janice Carlson, to his former partner, editor Phyllis Galde. This time the topic is aliens. Are they good or bad and what are their intensions? The answer is mixed, but generally good news. Most only want to help the human race, but beware the insectivores!

Fate magazine is available on newsstands or by subscription from fatemag.com

Giant
GUNSMOKE

FEATURING NEW STORIES BY:

A. B. Guthrie, Jr.
Frank O'Rourke
Jack Schaefer
Noel Loomis
Nelson Nye
Bill Gulick
Steve Frazee
Bennett Foster

ANC
35 CENTS

If you wandered in expecting Dillon and his ilk, you'd best move along, friend. This here *Gunsmoke* is a damned sight darker, dirtier and more brutal.

Gunsmoke
Article by Peter Enfantino

Gunsmoke featured gritty, realistic western stories written by the most respected writers of the day. The content mirrored that of its sister publication, the ground-breaking crime digest, *Manhunt* (1953–1967). Despite, or maybe because of, its darker edge, the digest was not successful enough to warrant more than a two-issue run. Based on the contents of the two issues published, that's a shame. This could have, eventually, become the most respected western digest published.

Another highlight carried over from *Manhunt* was *Gunsmoke*'s use of colorful biographies of its featured writers. It's hard to imagine in today's world of "reference at your fingertips," but there probably weren't too many places a reader could turn to find information on their favorite western writers. These short, often humorous (Bill Gulick admits that he's fond of vegetable gardening but his agent hates it) bits filled in some of the blanks.

After the two issues were published, many of the leftover copies were bound together and released as *Giant Gunsmoke*. It's not clear whether a third issue was planned and then scrapped, but it would seem the reasoning behind *Giant Gunsmoke* might have been to attract more readers. Whether or not that was the case, the plan didn't work[1]. At least

---

1 *Manhunt* issued thirteen of their *Giant Manhunt* omnibus editions (some of the volumes contained four issues bound together). *Alfred Hitchcock's Mystery Magazine* issued several volumes of *Alfred Hitchcock's Mystery Sampler*, which bound together two uncirculated copies of *AHMM*. The difference between the bound copies of *Manhunt* and those of *AHMM* is that the publishers of *Hitch* would bind random copies! I've heard stories from collectors of innumerable combinations of issues. It's not all that far-fetched since three of the four *Samplers* I have in my collection all contain non-consecutive issues.

we have two issues of a magazine that gave us several solid, and in a few cases classic, western tales.

Can't ask for more than that.

Vol. 1 No. 1 June 1953
144 pages, 35 cents

The Man with No Thumbs
by Noel Loomis
(7500 words) ★★☆

Jonas Marson is the no-nonsense leader of a bunch of Apache scalpers. The men kill Apaches and sell their scalps to the Mexican government. One night, Al Hobart, a former comrade of the bunch, staggers into camp with a tale of Indian torture. The fact that he's shown up minus both thumbs convinces every man he's telling the truth but Marson, who never liked Hobart in the first place and may have, in fact, fed him to the Indians. Hobart offers his tracking expertise to the gang and, despite warnings of a trap from Marson, they take him up on it. Turns out Marson is right and Hobart leads the men right into the hands of the Apaches. The finale finds Marson, staked naked across an anthill, the Apaches slowly skinning him alive, while Hobart watches gleefully.

This gruesome revenge yarn would have found a perfect home in Joe R. Lansdale's equally gruesome anthology of western horrors, *Razored Saddles*. "Thumbs" is liberally spiced with beheadings, disembowelments, and descriptive scalpings of women and children:

Hooker was down, scalping bodies. He yanked off a long, black-haired scalp with a loud pop, and held it up in the moonlight. "There's a woman here!" He screamed at Marson.

A door opened. A shot sounded. A groan. The door crashed in. Its rawhide hinges shrieked as they gave away. A woman screamed and there was another shot. Then children shrieked, and there was silence for an instant.

Jeff Sadler, in his entry on Noel Loomis in *Twentieth Century Western Writers*, says of the author: "Violence shapes the work of Noel M. Loomis. There is a savage force at work . . . evoking the atmosphere of a harsh, untamed land. His writing captures the taste and scent of another time." Indeed there is a gritty edge to Loomis' short stories, be it "Thumbs" or "When the Children Cry for Meat" (found in Greenberg and Pronzini's *The Texans*, Fawcett, 1988) or "A Decent Saddle" (from *Zane Grey's Western Magazine*, August 1953). Loomis also found success with such 1950s western novels as *Johnny Concho* (Gold Medal, 1956), *North to Texas* (Ballantine, 1956), and *The Leaden Cache* aka *Cheyenne War Cry* (Avon, 1959). Sadler sums up Loomis: "In the field he chose, he has yet to be surpassed."

Rock Bottom by Nelson Nye
(5000 words) ★★☆

Bank robber Jeff Farradine knows his obsession can get him killed. With a posse hot on his trail, Farradine hits the town of Rock Bottom, searching for the girl who has haunted his every waking moment, a girl he only caught a glimpse of months before. Convinced she'll drop everything to ride off into the sunset with him, Farradine spends hours scouring the town until he finds her. Of course, he's a bit surprised when he finds she's the town's favorite hooker at the local brothel. Convincing the girl (and attempt-

GUNSMOKE

EVERY STORY NEW!

JUNE
35 CENTS

NEWCOMER
By
A. B. Guthrie, Jr.

Plus — FRANK O'ROURKE · JACK SCHAEFER · NELSON NYE
STEVE FRAZEE · NOEL LOOMIS — and others

ing to convince himself as well) that her way of life will not hamper their relationship, they leave the cathouse, only to be confronted by the posse. Farradine is mowed down and his true love returns to her profession.

Interesting character study has the hardened bank robber/lifer criminal who truly believes he can drop his evil ways for the love of a woman. The author nicely counters with a hooker who doesn't necessarily want to leave her "tainted" life behind. In fact, she's very comfortable with her path.

Nelson Nye was an incredibly prolific western novelist during the four decades he wrote—with such classic paperbacks as *Rafe/Hideout Mountain* (Ace Double, 1962), *Bandido* (Signet, 1957), and *Iron Hand* (Ace, 1966) under his wide belt. Nye also served as the initial president of the Western Writers of America in 1953, won the coveted Spur Award for Best Western of 1959 (*Long Run*, McMillan, 1959), and edited the fine anthology, *They Won Their Spurs* (Avon, 1962).

The Crooked Nail
by Frank O'Rourke
(5400 words) ☆

Dan Morgan returns to the town where he and four of his buddies stole thousands of dollars worth of bonds. Dan never saw a penny though, because it disappeared, along with two of his partners. Seeking answers, and his share, he coaxes the truth from the man who was once his best friend and is now his betrayer.

Very slow, with an expository (involving the titular hardware) that defies logic and instead invites chuckles. O'Rourke wrote a batch of baseball novels and short stories in the 1950s. Some of his short western fiction was collected in *Ride West* (Ballantine, 1953) and *Hard Men* (Ballantine, 1956).

Thirst by John Prescott
(5000 words) ☆☆

Reakor assists two bank robbers in their getaway. Sensing a double cross, he murders them first and hightails it into the desert. Hot on his tail is the town's sheriff. Though the story itself is nothing to get excited about, the author manages to spice it up with some fine writing:

It was long after sun-up when they came upon the bodies at the hole. The buzzards and coyotes had been at work and it was not a pretty sight. The deputy was a hardy man, but his stomach was sometimes weak. He nearly vomited.

"Gawd almighty," he said, *blanching, with the muscles in his face drawn tight. "It always gets me when I see them eyeballs that way."*

"Good food for the buzzards," the sheriff said. *"I don't know why it is, but they always seem to like them eyes."*

Prescott wrote several western novels in the 1950s, including *The Renegade* (Bantam, 1956), *Wagon Train* (Bantam, 1956), and *Guns of Hell Valley* (Graphic, 1957). He won a Spur for Best Historical Novel for *Journey By the River* (Random House, 1954). Two of his short pulp western novels, "The Longriders" and "The Hard One" were reprinted by Tor in their Double Action Western Series in 1990.

**Gunsmoke Selects:
A Six Gun Salute** by Parke Dwight (500 words) Non-fiction feature about Mutual Broadcasting System's "Western Week."

Newcomer by A. B. Guthrie, Jr.
(3400 words) ☆☆☆

For some reason known only to himself, the town's black sheep, Chilter, just doesn't like the new school teacher, Mr. Ellenwood. Chilter makes this apparent several times until inevitably things turn violent and Mr. Ellenwood has to prove that even a school teacher can reach a breaking point. To protect his son, Lonnie, and himself, Ellenwood beats the man down. Our final glimpse at Ellenwood is not of a man satisfied, proud and boasting, but saddened at the turn of events.

Ellenwood would have been played by Gary Cooper and Jack Palance would have been a natural for Chilter, but *Shane* had just been made (and would be previewed in the following issue's "Gunsmoke's Movie of the Month".) Sure, it's the same kind of story, but I enjoyed it just the same. Again, a familiar story is invigorated by sharp writing and visuals:

Mr. Ellenwood was stepping forward, not back, stepping into the wicked whistle and cut of the quirt, his head up and his eyes fixed. There was a terrible rightness about him, a rightness so terrible and fated that for a minute Lonnie couldn't bear to look, thinking of Stephen stoned and Christ dying on the cross—of all the pale, good, thoughtful men foredoomed before the hearty.

Ironically, the following year Guthrie would win an Academy Award nomination for his screenplay for, you guessed it, *Shane*.

The Killing at Triple Tree
by Evan Hunter
(5250 words) ★★★★

The posse's ready to lynch the scum that raped and murdered the sheriff's wife. So why won't the lawman let the town have its fun? Evan Hunter shows that he's just as good at depicting violent life in the West as in the East. The final few paragraphs come fast and furious like a load of buckshot to your face, leaving an unforgettable vision in your mind. "The Killing at Triple Tree" could just as easily have been placed in *Manhunt* and fit in nicely.

Old Chief's Mountain
by Bryce Walton
(5320 words) ★★

The only survivors of an Indian massacre roam the desert in search of water: three soldiers and a scout. The scout is convinced that water is only a mountain away. His endless droning, "Cool water, cool sweet water" reminded me of the old *I Love Lucy* episode with the actor who repeatedly says "Slowly I turned, step by step . . ." Though the story didn't do much for me, it does contain some harrowing descriptions of what days in the desert without water will do to a man.

Bryce Walton isn't widely known for his westerns (in fact, there is no listing for Walton in *Twentieth Century Western Writers*), but published several dozen science fiction shorts (under his own name and several pseudonyms) in such digests as *If*, *Fantastic*, *Vortex* and *Future*; and dozens more crime stories in *Manhunt*, *Mike Shayne*, *Alfred Hitchcock* and *Pursuit*. *The Long Night* (Falcon Digest, 1952) is the only Walton novel I can find reference to.

Judd by Jack Schaefer
(6800 words) ★★★★

Judd Birkett sits on his porch and watches as all his neighbors pack up and move away. Only old Judd wants to stay and fight the state men who plan to flood the valley once the new dam is built. Judd's little shack stands smack dab in the middle of progress. He won't give in even after his property is condemned and law moves in to remove him. "Judd" works as both a nicely told morality play and as an analogy of the old west herded out by the new. The story concludes with the chilling images of the water flooding the valley and an old man who's left with only one way out.

Schaefer's claim to fame lies with his novel, *Shane*, perhaps the most acclaimed and influential (certainly, to this day, one of the most-borrowed western storylines of all time) western of the 20th Century. *Shane* was, of course, made into the equally acclaimed 1953 flick starring Alan Ladd and the viciously evil Jack Palance. Brian Garfield once wrote "(D)espite its pretensions *Shane* codified the essence of the Western, and it remains one of the few altogether towering movies of the genre."

Great Medicine by Steve Frazee (11,650 words) ☆☆

A Blackfoot Indian named Little Belly believes he can become all-powerful if he steals the "great medicine" from a risky adventurer. Though this is one of Frazee's most reprinted stories, it's one of my least favorites. Surprisingly (for a Steve Frazee story, that is), it's slow-moving and uninvolving.

The Gunny by Robert Turner (3200 words) ☆☆

Fred Maurer is a professional assassin hired to pick fights and win them. After his latest job is completed, the past seems to catch up with him and he's haunted by visions of the men he's cut down. Very ambiguous and confusing, and ultimately unsatisfying. Robert Turner (aka Roy Carroll) sold hundreds of mystery tales to the pulps and over 60 stories to crime digests such as *Manhunt, Pursuit, Hunted* and *Guilty*, including my favorite Turner title, "Frogtown Vengeance," in *Hunted* #2 (February 1955). *Manhunt's* bio on Turner states that he was an agent and an editor before turning to full-time writing because it "made less ulcers." Eleven of the eighteen stories collected in *Shroud 9* (Powell, 1970) originally appeared in *Manhunt*. Novels included *The Tobacco Auction Murders* (Ace, 1954), *Woman Chaser* and *Strange Sisters* (both Beacon, 1962), and *The Night is For Screaming* (Pyramid, 1960). Turner wrote a short piece on "The Not-So-Literary Digests" for *Xenophile* #38 (1978), wherein he opined that *Gunsmoke* died a quick death "probably because the typical western story fan didn't go for off-trail stories."

Gunsmoke's Movie of the Month:
Ambush at Tomahawk Gap
(100 words) Non-fiction feature.

The Boy Who Smiled
by Elmore Leonard
(5000 words) ☆☆☆☆

Mickey Segundo has carried a man-sized chip on his very young shoulder since the day he watched T.O. McKay and his men lynch Mickey's innocent father for no reason other than to watch him swing. Bad mistake on McKay's part leaving the boy to live. Mickey grows up enough to exact a terrible revenge ala Charles Bronson's character in Sergio Leone's *Once Upon a Time in the West*.

An engrossing tale that switches viewpoints at various stages. You can see the beginnings of a wonderful storyteller emerging from Elmore Leonard, and while he was best known for such crime novels as *Get Shorty, Out of Sight, Stick* and *Fifty-Two Card Pick Up*, he cut his writing teeth on the western. *The Bounty Hunters* (Ballantine, 1953) and *Escape from Five Shadows* (Dell, 1957) are every bit as dark and exciting as his crime fiction. Leonard's complete short stories were collected by Morrow in 2004 (*The Complete Western Stories of Elmore Leonard*), tales perfect for those who shun the genre because their idea of a western is Little Joe and Hoss.

Gunsmoke

Blue Chip Law
by Bill Erin
(1500 words) ★★★

Effective short-short about a mysterious poker player and the appointment he must keep at noon. The reader doesn't learn a lot in four pages (though there are several characters, we learn only the bartender's and the visitor's name) but the writing keeps it intriguing.

Vol. 1 No. 2 August 1953
144 pages, 35 cents

Final Payment by Frank O'Rourke
(10,500 words) ★★★★

Bill McKay has gone from troubled youth to murderous bank robber in record time. During one of his raids, he murders the father of his boyhood friend, Henry, now a big-time lawyer/politician in

Washington. McKay is captured but escapes a few years later and begins his bloody campaign anew. Collapsing under public outcry, Henry and the Governor concoct a plan: offer McKay a full pardon if he turns over the rest of his cutthroat gang to the law. McKay, festering the wounds of years of imprisonment and Henry, equally bitter over the loss of his father, finally meet face-to-face. Henry feels that there is something in Billy to be saved, but McKay's last laugh is to turn the lawyer over to his gang and bullets fly in a tense, exciting finale.

Unlike his previous *Gunsmoke* effort, "The Crooked Nail," "Final Payment" is every word a gripping, satisfying story (one told thousands of times in the western story) about two men whose hatred for each other threatens to engulf both of them. The reader can tell who wears the black hat and whom the white belongs to:

I was never over-possessed with courage and never foolhardiness; but I had inherited from my father and mother those principles of right and wrong they had lived by, and a stern, unbending belief in the fact that a man could not kneel to something false and cruel, and ever be a man again.

Sometimes I think that is the reason for all war, I don't know for sure, but it seems to have a grain of truth in its shell. I looked at Billy McKay and thought, "You poor, damned fool!" and remembered my father as he had been in life, unbending, often wrong, but never a coward.

The Hairy Mr. Fraily
by Jack Schaefer (7100 words) ★★

The ballad of Baldpate Fraily, the barber, and his two sons, Greenberry and Lenader. Not that this is a poorly-written fable, it's just that it doesn't belong in *Gunsmoke*, but rather a more varied digest like *Zane Grey's Western Magazine* or *Street & Smith's Western*. It's a change of pace but, for me at least, not a welcomed one.

Homecoming
by Nelson Nye
(4500 words) ★

Nor is this story, which belongs in *Ranch Romances*. Dode Rogers heads back to his hometown to clear his name and win back the love of his life, Tara Lord. Unlike Nye's "Rock Bottom" in the first issue (which is essentially the same story), the narrative of the story is driven into the ground by the weight of its own clichés, including this final exchange between the hero (picture James Brolin) and heroine (how about—think low budget here—Lindsay Wagner):

Tara said "Let's talk about us."

And Dode said, taking her into his arms, "The hell with talk."

No Guns by Louis Trimble
(4750 words) ★★★

Beeck and Herne are the Ali and Frazier of the town known as Vigilance, duking it out for years over the smallest of differences. But after two decades of blood and battles, Herne has an idea for a less combative relationship with Beeck. This humorous tale very much reminded me of Steve Frazee's short story "The Bretnall Feud" (first published in *Argosy* in 1953 and reprinted in the Bill Pronzini-edited *The Best Western Stories of Steve Frazee*), but with a much lighter tone and a "happier" ending. Trimble also wrote many mystery novels (*The Virgin Victim, The Corpse Without a Country*) and dabbled in science fiction as well (*Guardians of the Gate, The Bodelan Way*). Jon Clute, in *The Encyclopedia of Science Fiction* (St. Martin's, 1993) calls Trimble "extremely competent."

Owlhoot: Who's Who
by T. W. Raines (1000 words)
Gunsmoke's Movie of the Month: *Shane* (100 words)
Both are non-fiction pieces.

The Big Die-Up
by Steve Frazee
(5400 words) ★★★★

My two favorite "vintage" western writers are DeRosso and Frazee. I had heard a lot of good things about Frazee for years, so I picked up the novel *He Rode Alone* and found it engrossing, a noir western without the western trappings we've all become familiar with after watching way too many hours of *The Big Valley* and *Bonanza*. *He Rode Alone* is, in fact, a great Gold Medal revenge suspenser (ranking right up there with the best of Dan J. Marlowe, Peter Rabe and all the rest of the Gold Meddlers) that just happens to take place in the old west. Frazee could just have easily changed a few things and produced a contemporary crime novel.

Frazee's greatest strength is that his characters can make the staunchest Western detractor forget the western tag on the cover. He's also dark as hell. A lot of his characters don't end up better for their journeys and some don't make it at all.

"The Big Die-Up" offers up Jim Heister, a no-nonsense (but fair) rancher who's stacked plenty of hay in anticipation of a long and nasty winter. The other ranchers who make up the town hadn't been as foresighted and ride to Heister's door to demand he share the feed. Heister refuses, citing his own personal welfare, and the refusal touches off a series of events that opens Jim's eyes to the neighbors around him and personal responsibility to the community.

Frazee wastes no lines and packs a novel's worth of characterization into a dozen pages. Here's a sample (the first two paragraphs of the story):
With the warmth of the fireplace pressing against his back, Jim Heister looked east along the snow fields and saw them coming. They rode through the drifts like men with defeat upon them, and that could make them savage. Six of them. There might have been twelve, but some of the Great Park ranchers were too full of pride and some of them hated Heister too much to come begging.

He was a lean, tall man with a look of sharp assurance on his snow-burned features. He stood in the warmth of what was his and watched the snow trail away in streamers from the legs of the laboring horses that were carrying men to Whispering Pines on a futile mission.

Killer by H. A. DeRosso
(10,750 words) ★★★

If Steve Frazee dims the lamp a bit, then H. A. DeRosso shuts it out completely. Outside of Frazee, no one wrote gloomier tales of weak humans and the moral dilemmas they face than DeRosso. Take the story included here for instance. "Killer" concerns ex-sheriff Dan Baxter, who receives word from the town's new sheriff that Jesse Olivera has escaped from prison. Years before, Dan had hunted Olivera down for rustling and, in a violent shootout, had wounded Olivera and killed the rustler's wife. Olivera had sworn revenge on Baxter and was now obviously heading for town. Not one to wait for danger to find him, Baxter heads out in search of the fugitive. When he finds him, he gives the man the chance to avenge his wife's death, only to beat the man in a draw. As Olivera lies bleeding to death, he thanks Baxter for the chance. Bill Pronzini[2] calls "Killer": "a quintessential DeRosso noir vision." I agree with Bill that shades are dark, but to fully appreciate DeRosso, seek out "Vigilante," (originally from the September 1948 issue of *Best Western* and reprinted in the excellent DeRosso collection *Under the Burning Sun*), possibly the darkest western pulp story I've ever read.

Scalp Dance by Bennett Foster
(6000 words) ★★

Jebs Farnford is caught between the savagery of his wife's Sioux family and the law-abiding "decency" of his own. When his ranch is hit hard by rustlers, Jebs must choose which tact to take. Strange, meandering narrative never quite involves the reader.

Behind the Badge:
Billy Tilghman by M. L. Powell (1000 words) non-fiction piece

Snowblind
by Evan Hunter
(3500 words) ★★

Gary finds his son Bobby sparking up a smoke, toting his guns, and anticipating a ride into town to get himself some sack time. Not ready for middle age and the sudden maturity of his offspring, Gary does the only thing that comes to mind: he grounds the kid. This doesn't sit well with the teen rebel and he grabs a hunk of the highway, just in time for one of those damned blizzards to hit. Feeling guilty for clipping the kid's wings, Gary sets out to track Bobby and is kidnapped by three ornery cusses wanted by the law for . . . something. In the eye-opening (for Gary at least—the rest of us know what's coming, right?) finale, father is saved by his gunslingin' son. The lesson here, of course, is that in the Old West you grew up faster and old people just had to accept that. The final paragraph finds the two-unit family looking forward to a cup of Joe, a roll-yer-own and, presumably, a threesome with Madame Kitty.

The Courting Feud
by Bill Gulick
(5500 words) ★★★

Judd Kimbrough and Henry Hooker are engaged in a game of one-upmanship while courting Molly Rankin. Light and humorous, very much like one of those 1950s western/romances, complete with musical interlude.

---

2 Bill Pronzini has done more to bring vintage western writers to a wider contemporary audience than anyone else. His "Best of the West" series for Fawcett in the 1980s reprinted over a hundred western stories formerly languishing in moldy pulps, including work by authors discussed in this piece. Bill is also responsible for a series of books reprinting the best of H. A. De Rosso: *Under the Burning Sun* (1997), *Riders of the Shadowlands* (1999) and *Tracks in the Sand* (2001), all published by Five Star.

Incident at the Bar W
by Robert Turner
(3250 words) ★★★

Esther Womble has only her dog to protect her when a stranger comes riding into her ranch. When the rider decides to take more than just the water he's been offered, Esther shows him how women survive in the West.

Showdown
by Charles Beckman, Jr.
(1250 words) ★★

Dave Segel has waited over two years for August Lehman's bullet to take him down. He can't eat, can't sleep, can't rest. He lives in constant fear. Then, finally, one night Lehman catches up to him, or does he? In one of those O. Henry type twists that might have been fresher when the story was first published, we find out that Segel actually killed Lehman years before and, plagued by guilt, turns to booze and sees his victim everywhere he turns. We learn this in the clichéd finale at the climax.

Sources
Garfield, Brian *Western Films* (Rawson Associates, 1982)
Sadler, Geoff (editor) *Twentieth Century Western Writers*, 2nd Edition (St. James Press, 1991)
Pronzini, Bill *The Best Western Stories of Steve Frazee* (Southern Illinois University Press, 1984)

Further Reading
DeRosso, H. A. *44* (Lion, 1953) *Under the Burning Sun* (Five Star, 1997)
Frazee, Steve *The Gun-Throwers* (Lion, 1954) *Pistolman* (Lion, 1952)
Gorman, Ed (editor) *The Fatal Frontier* (Carroll & Graf, 1997)
Loomis, Noel *Heading West* (Leisure, 2007)

Peter Enfantino is an obsessive collector of Mystery, Crime and Horror digests including *Alfred Hitchcock, Manhunt, Mike Shayne*, as well as the entire stable of Warren Magazines. He has written for all the major channels on the topics, including *Paperback Parade, Mystery Scene, Mystery File, Comic Effect*, and Peter Normanton's *From the Tomb*. For thirteen years he co-edited *The Scream Factory* and *Bare Bones* magazines, and currently blogs at bare·bones e-zine. He divides his time between Mesa, AZ and London, England.

"Ain't got no Mr. Dillon, ain't got no Miss Kitty, no wonder it only lasted two issues."

Social Intercourse

Engage! Poke a keyboard and make some meaningful interactions on or offline.

The Digest Enthusiast book two with Joe Wehrle, Jr.'s cover painting

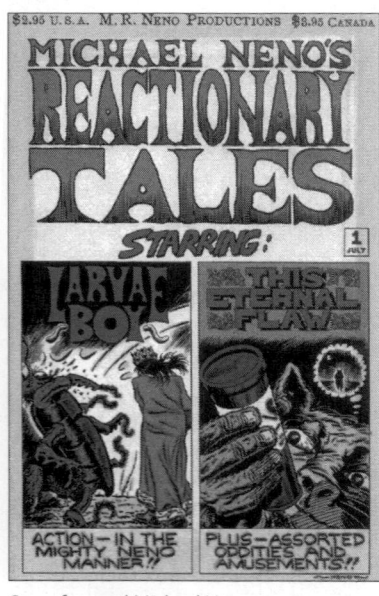

One of several Michael Neno comics available at nenoworld.com

Many thanks to everyone who wrote, reviewed or rated *TDE2*. John O'Neill wrote on Black Gate: "I especially appreciated the reviews of current digests, which I found well written and enthusiastic." Thank you John, we'll make it a point to review old and new titles/issues each outing.

One aspect of *TDE* that Rob Lott emphasized in his review on Bookgasm, was discovery: "Joe Wehrle Jr.'s article on a long-running action-comics digest from Italy, starring eponymous he-man *Mister No*. Where else would we learn of such a thing on this side of the globe?" Initially, the digest format seemed like an artificial dividing line for a magazine about genre fiction, but the range of titles and subject matter proved otherwise. Part of the fun is discovering another title I had no idea existed—and then finding an expert who can tell us all about it.

I had the pleasure of attending Bouchercon 2015 in October and finally had a chance to meet D. Blake Werts, who drove from Charlotte to Raleigh. At the con, I connected with Bill Crider, Robert Lopresti and Dana King, among others; and

Visit roblopresti.com for links and background on his latest novel, *Greenfellas*.

Keep up with Ron Fortier's numerous projects at airship27.com

attended four days of panel discussions with an amazing roster of crime fiction writers. My favorite panel moment was at the "Masters in Crime & Mystery" session with Bill Crider and Lawrence Block. When asked for their favorite reading guilty pleasures, Bill cited paperback originals and digests, and Lawrence said, "digests like *Sure Fire, Off Beat.*" Music to my ears gentlemen!

Bill is a great supporter of our efforts. In his post about *TDE2* on his Pop Culture Magazine, he wrote, "Interviews, articles, reviews, stories, you just can't go wrong. I highly recommend it."

Gary Lovisi, editor of *Paperback Parade* wrote about *TDE* in issue #90: "This is a welcome new magazine in our field." I only wish we could match the frequency of Gary's fine magazine!

Ron Fortier posted his review about *TDE2* on Amazon as well as his blog, Pulp Fiction Reviews: "Being a writer/editor, the latter [short fiction] has particular appeal to me . . ." The main event in virtually all of the digests we write about is genre fiction so it seems appropriate to include a

For a good time visit billcrider.blogspot.com

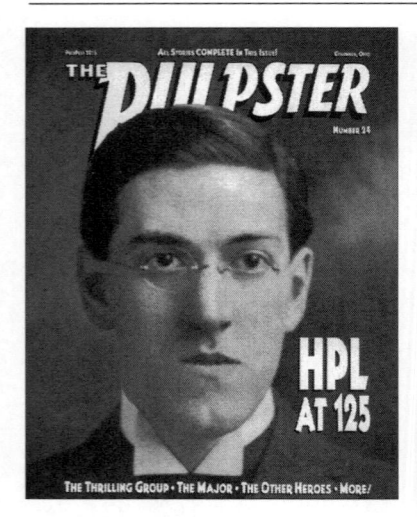

Mike Chomko's *The Pulpster* is available at sites.google.com/site/mikechomkobooks/

Visit gryphonbooks.com for the full library of Gary Lovisi's novels and magazines.

few stories in our book as well.

James Reasoner noted on Rough Edges: "... I've gone back and ordered the first issue so I can catch up...." Much appreciated, James. Although our sales remain low we have seen some incremental growth since issue #2. Thus far *TDE1* has outsold *TDE2* by about 33% and our delivery split is 66% print, 33% digital, which tracks true for both editions.

Pulp fans are well aware of Bill Thom's essential Pulp Coming Attractions website. Bill gave us excellent support on *TDE2* and the launch of our blog on larquepress.com

Jack Rems, Ron Kayo and Mike Chomko invested in *TDE* with copies for sale in their bookstores, shows and mail order businesses. Thanks for giving *TDE* a presence there.

On the social media front, additional support for *TDE2* was posted on Amazon, Facebook, Goodreads or other social sites. This includes Steve Alcorn of the writingacademy.com, voracious reader John Adkins, Terry K., Mark Rose, J. Cassara, writer/artist Michael Neno, author Robert Lopresti, Steve Darnall of *Nostalgia Digest*, and Maurice, who rated *TDE1* on Amazon.uk. (If I've inadvertently missed you, it wasn't intentional.) Your words are far more useful to potential readers than ours.

Digests featured on the back cover this issue include:
Gunsmoke #1 June 1953
Super-Science Fiction
  Vol. 3 #4 June 1959
Big Fiction #2 Spring/Summer 2012
Diabolik March 2015
Bestseller Mystery B40, June 15, 1943
Beyond Vol. 2 #11, July 1969

Plans for *TDE4* include Tom Brinkmann's report on Criswell's column for *Spaceway Science Fiction*, an article about *Suspense* (squeezed out of this issue) and much more.
    -RK

Opening Lines

Select openings from yesterday's digest magazines.

"He stumbled about the kitchen trying to wake up at the godless hour of six in the morning, a time when only birds, idiots, hangovers and outdoor type women bestirred themselves."
"Black Birds of Doom" by Bryce Walton
Off Beat Detective Stories, Nov. 1958

"Donnie sat in his beat-to-shit Pinto with the heater on full, huddling for warmth beneath the driver's-side window that wouldn't quite shut. An icy wind whipped through the half-inch gap, numbing his hands as he checked the .38 Special."
"Clean-Up on Aisle 3" by Adam Howe
Thuglit #19 Sept/Oct 2015

"Mark Smeaton hurried through the darkened London streets, his nimble feet executing frivolous little dance steps as he went. They carried him onto the rotting boards of the small pier which jutted out into the Thames."
"Murder: Scene One" by Denham Kelsey
Web Terror Stories, February 1965

"It was getting harder and harder to bring Stella to weddings. With each ceremony she had grown wilder, and behavior that had once been mischievous now vaulted into recklessness, unruliness, and outright vandalism. Three weeks ago, at the Harris-Watson wedding, Ted caught her scrawling her name on the side of the wedding cake with her fingernail, and only by chance had he been able to sneak her out of the room and smooth out the fondant without anyone noticing."
"I'll Be your Forever" by Panio Gianopoulos
Big Fiction #7

"The reward was three G's. If you've a Caddy and a town house, or even a Chevvy and a bungalow, you won't risk your neck for that sort of green. I've two kids and a wife who never complains, but when I see margarine on the table, I know that Ellen first looked at the butter."
"Protection Break" by Alex Jackinson
The Man From U.N.C.L.E. August 1966

"The famous TV comedian, Jackie Gleason, although few people know it, is very much interested in psychic phenomena. He is a subscriber to *Search*, as well as to every other psychic magazine published."
"Jackie Gleason, Psychic Investigator"
Search Magazine #21 June 1957

"The house was of red brick, large and square, with a green slate roof, whose wide overhang gave the building an appearance of being too squat for its two stories; and it stood on a grassy hill, well away from the country road, upon which it turned its back to look down on the Mokelumne River."
"Night Shots" by Dashiell Hammett
Bestseller Mystery B81 "Hammett Homicides" Dec. 20, 1946

"As we were watching the ionosphere and luminous clouds at the observation station in Oege, Latvia, on July 26, 1965, we noticed at 9:35 p.m. an extremely bright star which seemed to be slowly moving westwards."
"Soviets Finally Confess UFO Sightings" by Timothy Green Beckley
Beyond July 1969

Printed in Great Britain
by Amazon